Mike Massé brilliantly  toral heart shares the eration so desperate for the depth of walking with God. His practical message brings deep truths into a culture that has in many ways abandoned these solid foundations of living. I am extremely grateful that he is providing the Body of Christ with a sustainable source of building character while avoiding the legalistic traps that so often can filter through these subjects. Well done! Great Book!

—DANNY STEYNE
APOSTOLIC LEADER, MOUNTAIN OF WORSHIP
TOLLAND, CT

(Prepare to) take a journey with my friend Mike Massé. You will definitely laugh, and probably cry. You will need to pause and re-read some sections and meditate. In the process, if you apply what you are reading, you will increasingly become who you are.

—FROM THE FOREWORD BY JUSTIN KENDRICK
LEAD PASTOR OF CITY CHURCH AND HOLYFIRE MINISTRIES
NEW HAVEN, CT

Mike has delivered a fresh look at some of the most vital areas of knowing and living for God. This home-run hit captivates with his straightforward approach. I highly encourage you to apply these principles that are sure to be a game-changer in your life.

—JACOB OUELLETTE
LEAD PASTOR OF THRIVE CHURCH
PARKER, CO

I really, really like this book. Mike has some great thoughts, and a wonderful way of bringing them.

—DR. BRIAN SIMMONS
TRANSLATOR, THE PASSION TRANSLATION OF THE BIBLE

Tina,

You bring His joy to your
Father and other people. I bless your
gift of joy + continued revelation of daughtership!

MC

#iamholy

Mike Massé

CREATION
HOUSE

#IAMHOLY by Mike Massé
Published by Creation House
A Charisma Media Company
600 Rinehart Road
Lake Mary, Florida 32746
www.charismamedia.com

Design Director: Bill Johnson
Cover design by Nathan Morgan

Visit the author's website: www.iamholy.net

Library of Congress Cataloging-in-Publication Data:
2013957320
International Standard Book Number: 978-1-62136-721-5
E-book International Standard Book Number:
978-1-62136-722-2

While the author has made every effort to provide accurate telephone numbers and Internet addresses at the time of publication, neither the publisher nor the author assumes any responsibility for errors or for changes that occur after publication.

First edition

14 15 16 17 18 — 9 8 7 6 5 4 3 2 1
Printed in Canada

DEDICATION

*Becca—my wife, my Ruth, my perfect
one—for running after Him with me. The
grace conversion that inspired this book
has actually made our marriage as close to
paradise as we get this side of eternity... and
the best is yet to come. I love you!*

TABLE OF CONTENTS

FOREWORD

THROUGHOUT THE HISTORY of the Church it seems that God allows for certain messages at certain times to spark spiritual awakening among his people. During the Reformation it was the message of justification by faith. During the Great Awakening it was the message of the new birth. God doesn't change but his people do. We forget things. We lose track of things. We are in need of constant redirecting.

There is a temptation to think about Bible stories like we think about good movies. They're entertaining, thought provoking, and may carry some solid life lessons, but the people in them seem larger than life. We read about David, Samson, Jesus, and Peter, and we treat them like characters rather than real people. This attitude causes us to forget that we are currently living in the middle of God's story. God is just as active in our time as he was in their time. History is not a random smattering of events. It's leading somewhere. God is landing this plane.

So, if we really are a part of this story of God, then what is God doing in our lifetime?

The Gospel of John tells us that the law was given through Moses, but *grace* and *truth* came through Jesus Christ. Grace and truth. Remember that: Grace and truth.

It seems that the history of the Church has been a process of rediscovering grace and truth. Our first misstep was to lose track of truth. After the resurrection of Jesus and compilation of the New Testament, it wasn't long before truth was taken out of the hands of his followers. Christians were taught to believe that the scripture was only to be read by the spiritually elite. Thanks to Martin Luther (who translated the Bible into the language of the common people) and Johannes Gutenberg (who figured out a way to mass produce it), and many other saints, truth was re-introduced to the Church. Today, you can read the Bible in NIV, ESV, NLT, AMP, MSG, or NKOTB. We have access to God's truth.

The Devil is as real as he was in the Garden of Eden and he's aware of the power of God's grace and truth in Jesus. As soon as he could no longer restrict humanity's access to the truth, he directed his efforts to the distortion and misappropriation of grace. God has already broken through Satan's plan and provided access to the truth for his Church. In our time, God is once again tearing apart the plans of Satan and revealing *grace* to his people.

What is the nature of grace? Is it a free pass to sin again and again? Not hardly. It is power beyond human ability to regenerate the heart and transform our desires. It is a new identity, rooted in the person of Jesus. It is the power to be forever fully forgiven; blameless before God. Grace provides the opportunity to come as close to the Father as Jesus the Son can come. What must we give to access this type of grace?

Nothing.

And everything.

In the words of the late Dietrich Bonhoeffer, "*Such grace is costly because it calls us to follow, and it's grace because it calls us to follow Jesus Christ. It is costly because it costs a man his life, and it is grace because it gives a man the only true life. It is costly because it condemns sin, and grace because it justifies the sinner. Above all, it is costly because it cost God the life of his Son."* (*The Cost of Discipleship*, p. 45).

God's salvation by grace through faith is the treasure in the field (Matt 13:44). The guy who found the treasure didn't earn it and didn't deserve it, but in response to it he joyfully sold all that he had and bought the field. This is amazing grace. Free and costly.

In the following pages you will take a journey with my friend Mike Massé. You will definitely laugh, and probably cry. You will need to pause and re-read some sections and meditate. In the process, if you apply what you are reading, you will increasingly *become who you are.*

Let God do a work in your heart. Let him rearrange everything. History demands that in our time we discover the beauty and power of God's grace. Learn it. Love it. Live from it. Find your identity in the face of Jesus.

Humbled by grace,

—Justin Kendrick
Founder of Holyfire Ministries
Lead Pastor of City Church
New Haven CT

ACKNOWLEDGMENTS

I OWE EVERYTHING TO Jesus for His #firstlove. In addition to my wife, God used several other people as catalysts that caused me to search the Word—in a place of intimacy with Jesus—that began the barrage of truth summed up in this book. The primary source was the teachings of Dan Mohler. Several concepts in this book are paraphrased based on how I heard Dan say it first via podcast. The other big influences on #iamholy are the sermon series "Process of Maturity" by Graham Cooke, Derek Levendusky's book "Discipleship by Grace," Justin Kendrick's teaching on liberty from the Brave Generation 2013 conference, online conversations with Joey Giuffrida, live conversations with Jonathan Bartlett, and of course sitting for more than five years under the preaching and mentoring of Weston and Karen Brooks.

My kids, Micah and Josiah Talon, for playing quietly while Daddy wrote. Well that might be a stretch...but I can give you a shout out for loving me through the entire process.

My parents, D. Michael (Coach) and Sharron Massé, for their prayers and encouragement throughout my life.

My in-laws, Rick and Yvonne Martin for their support and blessings these last few years.

The teens from the Rising for their constant inspiration. I couldn't be prouder of you.

Everyone at River of Life, you stir my heart to love and good works.

Everyone who donated to the Indiegogo project (or just handed me a check!)—this book could not have been completed without you guys. You are part of something amazing, spreading a message of freedom and victory for God's sons and daughters worldwide! A special mention to those who donated $50 or more: Dave Scioscio, Christopher Dutton, Kristian Tedford, Anthony and Krista Billard, David Gebel, Nate and Christina Desjardins, Rachel Bartlett, Michelle Suizdak (and several others who demanded to remain anonymous). #iamverygrateful

Introduction
HE IS I AM

I AM HOLY"? *THAT'S more arrogant than "I am Iron Man!"*

Thanks for the encouragement. We actually address the pride issue in Chapter 1, but we have to establish first off, this is all about God. One of the coolest moments in the Bible occurs when they try to tell Jesus about how He's no Abraham, and He responds with: "Before Abraham was born, I AM." Goose bumps! That's a pretty clear reference to when God told Moses "I AM." No further explanation needed. #iamholy comes down to identity. And our identity is found *completely* in Him.

Two extreme mind-sets exist that oppose what we want to accomplish in this book. Both will be discussed as we go, but just to get the ball rolling: there's *legalism*, which says about our holiness, in essence, "We can never be holy. God is great, but we will always be cesspools of wickedness." On the other side, *license* basically states: "I am awesome just because I exist. I can think, say, and do whatever I want...and because God is nice, He'll be cool with it, and I will still be considered holy."

I thought it would be a good idea to get both errors out of the way before going any further. The best way to do that is to expose our hearts to several scriptures that show us the truth. Everything that this book reveals "I am" comes only from God, the great "I AM."

Who is like unto thee, O Lord, among the gods?
Who is like thee, *glorious in holiness*, fearful in
praises, doing wonders?
—Exodus 15:11, kjv, emphasis added

There is none holy as the Lord; for there is none
beside thee.
—1 Samuel 2:2, kjv

The Lord is righteous in all His ways, and holy in
all His works.
—Psalm 145:17, kjv

We get the picture, right? God is inherently holy, righteous,
pure, glorious—we can establish that these are unchanging
truths about the Lord. Few would argue this point.

Now, does He want us to do anything with the revelation that He is holy? Let's check back in the Word:

"You are to be holy to me [or *"be my holy ones"*]
because I, the Lord, am holy, and I have set you
apart from the nations to be my own."
—Leviticus 20:26, emphasis added

That seems pretty clear. Many denominations don't
accept a command from the Old Testament unless it's
confirmed in the New Testament. Challenge accepted!

As obedient children, do not be conformed to the
passions of your former ignorance, but as he who
called you is holy, you also *be holy in all your conduct*, since it is written, *"You shall be holy, for I am
holy."*
—1 Peter 1:14–16, esv, emphasis added

Again, most would find it hard to argue that verse as vague or confusing. It seems to be a clear confirmation that the Lord wants us to be holy as He is holy. But since we never want to be accused of taking one or two verses out of context...

> *No one who abides in him keeps on sinning; no one who keeps on sinning has either seen him or known him.* Little children, let no one deceive you. *Whoever practices righteousness is righteous, as he is righteous. Whoever makes a practice of sinning is of the devil,* for the devil has been sinning from the beginning. The reason the Son of God appeared was to destroy the works of the devil. *No one born of God makes a practice of sinning, for God's seed abides in him, and he cannot keep on sinning because he has been born of God.* By this it is evident who are the children of God.
> —1 JOHN 3:6–10, ESV, EMPHASIS ADDED

> Make every effort to live in peace with all men and to *be holy*; without *holiness* no one will see the Lord.
> —HEBREWS 12:14, EMPHASIS ADDED

As my high school geometry teacher always used to say: "Mike, pay attention!" Sorry, I was looking for her second-most-quoted statement: "It's a given." We have now established by several passages from both Testaments that 1) God is holy, and 2) Because of #1, we are to be holy.

How? Well, that's what the entirety of this book unpacks. But we have to start with the Word:

> Everyone who has this *hope in him* purifies himself, just as he is pure.
> —1 JOHN 3:3, EMPHASIS ADDED

The Kingdom of God is within you!
— LUKE 17:21, KJV, EMPHASIS ADDED

He who unites himself with the Lord is one with Him in spirit. . . . your body is a temple of the Holy Spirit, who is in you, whom you have received from God.
— 1 CORINTHIANS 6:17–19, EMPHASIS ADDED

Those who love me [Jesus] will obey my teaching. My Father will love them, and *my Father and I will come to them and live with them.*
— JOHN 14:23, EMPHASIS ADDED

I have been crucified with Christ; and *it is no longer I who live, but Christ lives in me*; and the life which I now live in the flesh I live by faith in the Son of God, who loved me and gave Himself up for me.
— GALATIANS 2:20, NASB, EMPHASIS ADDED

I love me some NASB . . . but sometimes, you just have to pull out The Passion Translation. Let's look at that last verse one more time:

My old life was crucified with Christ and no longer lives; for I was fully united with Him in His death. And now the essence of this new life is no longer mine, for Christ lives His life through me! My new life is empowered by the faith of the Son of God who loves me so much that HE gave Himself for me, and dispenses His life into mine!
— GALATIANS 2:20, TPT, EMPHASIS ADDED

Amen. My life is no longer mine, for Christ lives His life through me. All these things we have tried really hard to accomplish are already inside us because they are found in Him. That's why the Word doesn't simply tell us to "do holy things." It tells us to "be holy." #iamholy comes down to recognizing Jesus has already done it all in His death and resurrection. Our part is to cooperate with Him in the areas that will naturally manifest as His finished work becomes our focus. This book goes into depth regarding the specific areas of holiness/freedom, love, happiness, devotion/passion, victory/courage, power, and humility.

Does an effective way to grow in any or all of those areas sound good? You've come to the right place.

Chapter 1
I AM HOLY?

Y OU'RE KIDDING, RIGHT? *God alone is holy! I'm just a sinner saved by grace.*

I like that you're less sarcastic than the heckler from the introduction, but I have to question if you actually read the introduction. Either way, stay with me here. Those are, in a sense, accurate statements. In fact, I lived and preached them for about fifteen years. Because of that grace you mention, my life and ministry actually did produce some lasting fruit during that time. Far less, however, than you would think.

"God alone is holy" makes a pretty solid statement, but we tend to attach some unfortunate (and unbiblical) connotations to it. "I'm just a sinner saved by grace"—while partially correct and widely accepted as the thrust of the gospel—is sadly incomplete. Let's revisit that thought in a few moments.

The whole idea for this book came out of an unscripted comment during a message delivered one night at the Rising (the student ministry my wife and I pastor). As has become the norm, I made an off-the-cuff joke that was mildly funny. This time, though, I failed to foresee a mildly risqué double meaning that elicited a few extra giggles in the back of the room. Immediately, I realized where their minds had gone and clarified the fact that *that* particular interpretation hadn't even crossed mine.

1

Speaking from the heart, I punctuated my brief explanation with "I am holy."

Talk about huge. The joke long forgotten, I found myself floored by that statement. As recently as *one year* earlier, that statement (spoken by any preacher, let alone yours truly) would have come across to me as incredibly arrogant.

But there it stood—a confident declaration void of any sinful pride. It came instead from a place of humble surrender to Christ in me, the hope of glory. "I am holy" had become part of who I was.

Where did that revelation come from? I had spent fifteen years of striving to live more like Jesus with mixed (but mostly frustrating) results. Yet a change had certainly taken place over the previous year or so that led to a life that manifested holiness with none of the former striving.

Derek Levendusky calls this shift a grace conversion (the description I will typically use). Leif Hetland titles it a love baptism. Regardless of what terminology you prefer, it's simply a wholehearted realization that our heavenly Father sees us not based on our past or current performance, but based on the finished work of Jesus Christ.

GOOD NEWS FOR THOSE WHO DON'T CURRENTLY FOLLOW JESUS

The Word makes it clear that there is *no condemnation* in Christ Jesus. If you have never put your faith in God, keep reading. You're in for a fun ride. One of my main goals is to destroy the biggest misconception many people have about Christianity: basically, that it's a list of fun-killing rules practiced by hypocrites. Nothing could be further from the truth. I bring the #iamholy perspective and lifestyle everywhere I go, and it's been awesome seeing people respond to it.

For instance, the old friend that recently heard I was a pastor. Him: Oh, I know how that goes. I guess you had to really clean yourself up for *that* crowd! Me: Nope, not at all. Him: Wait, what? Me: I couldn't clean myself up if I tried. Could you?

This led to an amazing conversation about what really happens when you become a Christian, ending with him asking if he could come to church with me that weekend!

CONDEMNATION VS. OPPORTUNITY

If you have already put your faith in Jesus, you're still in for a fun ride—but let's make it clear up front that nothing in this book should make you feel condemned, ashamed, like you're not measuring up, or that you "don't get it." Everything presented here that anyone is not yet walking in should be seen as an opportunity. We tend to turn defensive every time an idea contrary to what we have always been taught gets raised. One of the things I laid down after my grace conversion was the need to be "right." You can disagree, or even start a blog called "More like #iamaheretic," and all I'll do in return is love you. But I encourage you to prayerfully and in the light of God's Word consider everything said here. Weigh it piece by piece against what you currently practice and start walking out any piece that leads to more freedom, joy, and holiness in Him.

See, there will be a ton of Scripture quoted in this book. But you will notice that every concept explained here that doesn't have an official Bible reference may seem familiar. That's because it's been saturated in the Word. Everything I write, based on everything I walk out, has been birthed in a place of poring over God's truth and a place of intimacy with Jesus.

RECITING BIBLE VERSES VS. LIVING OUT THEIR TRUTHS

Memorization certainly has a place. But we've entered a time best exemplified by what Jamie LaFond says: "Don't show me the fifty Bible verses you've memorized. Show me the one you are living!" She's a wise woman; and someone even wiser—Jesus Himself—said, "You are in error because you do not know the Scriptures...or the power of God!" I don't believe that means we merely need to memorize more. I believe it means we will see the Word manifest through our lives when we start seeing those truths from a heart that knows God's power and grace to live them!

I've always defined myself as a Bible and character guy, but I think we can all finally admit that being able to recite verses and defining character as a list of things we don't do simply does not work.

Again, study has its value. I mean, I possess a theology degree! But 99 percent of the people I minister to daily don't know or care about my exegetical credentials. The middle and high school youth at the Rising know the concepts of sanctification and justification; but what really transforms their lives is the revelation that they are sons and daughters of a king who created them to manifest His glory!

GOOD/BAD TREES AND FRUIT—A NEW PERSPECTIVE

Anyone familiar with church has probably heard the quote "You shall be known by your fruit." Maybe some of us—like me in college—have attended some services where it seemed like Jesus actually said, "You shall be known by your *suit.*" Yes, I've waited over a decade to unleash that joke…and I haven't seen anyone wear a suit to church since. But you're picking up what I'm putting down.

Dan Mohler raises a whole new understanding about this teaching of Christ on trees and fruit.[1] We hear "a good tree bears good fruit, a bad tree bears bad fruit," and have always taken it to mean "good Christians will have holy lives, bad Christians will have sin issues." Then we immediately fall into condemnation when we think on those issues that currently exist in our lives. We often take on the role of fruit inspectors, trying to improve external behaviors in ourselves. Even more often, we look around and wish others would work on their issues. Our ultimate goal is to be a good Christian, but we can take some solace in the fact that we're doing better than many other people at church by comparing fruit!

But what did Jesus actually say? A good tree can only bear good fruit. Instead of focusing on those less than stellar behaviors, grab hold of the truth that through Christ in me, *I am a good tree*, and watch what happens! When we understand that #iamholy already in my position before God through His grace, it is no surprise that holier "fruit" naturally results.

TODAY REALLY, REALLY IS THE FIRST DAY OF THE REST OF YOUR LIFE

All of us who have been in church for a while have been through phases where we heard a message by a certain minister, or read a book on a theme that excited us. Whatever it was each time, it consumed our thoughts for days, weeks, or even months afterward. Every devotional time in the Word, every conversation we had about the things of God centered on that theme. We got excited about living it out. Eventually, they each get filed away, remembered fondly, but replaced by the next "now" word for our faith journey.

#iamholy is different. It's a completely new mindset, although it's based on timeless truths. It's like a line gets crossed and you can never go back to the old way. Everything looks and gets lived out differently forever after God's grace gets a hold of your heart. For me, I felt like after fifteen years as a born-again, Spirit-filled Christian I actually saw the completeness of God's plan for the first time.

Please understand that "complete" doesn't mean having attained full maturity, wisdom, or understanding anywhere close to everything about God and His ways. It just means I now see the big picture of the gospel. He thought I was valuable enough to offer the life of His Son to get sin off me and holiness in me. And there are few things more exciting than seeing others get that revelation as well.

After fifteen years of trying just about everything to get teens to "be more consistent Christians," we actually see that very thing happen as we expose them to their true identity in Christ! We are seeing middle and high school students living victoriously for the first time. This doesn't mean sinless perfection or even adult-like "maturity." It means they have crossed the line into His grace and are starting to practice viewing themselves from the perspective of what Jesus did and not what they have or haven't done. They have begun to define themselves by who God says they are and not what their peers or ungracious authority figures say about them. An immediate benefit is getting to a point where stuff that happens to them does not dictate their emotional response anymore. I talk about many amazing specific things that we have seen in the lives of these youth in Chapter 7.*

BUT I'M ALWAYS GOING TO BE A SINNER THIS SIDE OF HEAVEN, RIGHT?

In church, at Christian college, even at some youth ministry conferences, I heard teaching and saw people live with what on the surface looks like humility. Christians proclaiming statements such as, "I'm nothing, He's everything." Prayers prayed publically that basically said, "I'm a worm and I have no idea why God would love wicked little me." Even whole messages devoted to the concept of "A wretch like me"! (Spoiler alert: that's not the name of the song. That would be "Amazing Grace.")

Let's get this out of the way right now. There is a moment where we need to come to a realization that our way doesn't work. You know, the "confess our sins" moment. I arrive at an understanding that I not only was born into, but also willingly entered with Adam and Eve into the sin nature. This put me in "wretch" territory. I admit how depraved I am when left to my own devices; I acknowledge that I have lived as a slave to sinful desires, and ultimately cannot save myself. I realize that Edwards, Moody, and other men and women whom God used mightily did use this information to help lead people to repentance...and it certainly has its place in presenting the full gospel to those who may be ignorant of it.

But here's my focus in this book and a big part of my

---

* Just so we understand how I sometimes mention being saved for a certain amount of time, i.e. fifteen years, and in other places talk about being in ministry for that same amount of time: I actually began as a volunteer in youth ministry before I truly gave my life to Christ. It's a long story, but powerful—ask me about it sometime!

life message: what causes one to renounce this way of life and change his or her purpose? I like to refer to the Bible for important answers, and mine says the kindness of God led me to repentance. The realization that during every moment I lived as His enemy, He loved me intensely enough to die for me is what breaks my heart and bends my knee before Him.

Then, that revelation leads me to put my faith in Jesus as Lord and Savior. I recognize His gift of grace that I have accessed through belief alone, that the old sinful "me" has now died and I am, in the words of the Messiah, "born again." Because I have laid down my life, it's no longer I that live, but Jesus actually now lives in and through me. I have officially become a new creation.

At that moment, *I stop being a wretch!* Jesus, undefeated against sin for the last *infinity* years, now lives in and through me. Dare I say…I am holy?

That's the issue that I have with claiming I'm "just a sinner saved by grace." I used to be a sinner. Used to be! That's past tense. I thank God He loved me when I was still a sinner. But even though His grace still saves me every hour of every day, my identity is no longer "sinner." He adopted me as His son. He only sees me through the finished work of Christ.

"Well, I'm nothing without Jesus." We've established that. Good thing I am not currently—nor will I be for one moment the rest of my life—without Jesus!

How Long Has it Been Since Your Last Confession, My Son?

"But I need to confess all of my sins every day to make sure I'm walking in purity. I can even back that practice up with

a Scripture verse or two!" My friend, I love that your heart
is to walk pure, but Weston Brooks (my pastor and a spiritual father) rightly raises this question: If purity is dependent on confessing each and every sin, what happens if
you accidentally or unconsciously miss one?

If this constant confession and "repentance" works
for you, please contact me on Twitter. I have yet to meet
someone who has attained real holiness this way. I have,
however, seen literally hundreds abandon their faith when
they realize the impossibility of this task. I once heard a
preacher talk about his childhood experience of "repentance" at the altar every Sunday morning at church. He
said not only would they have to cover every sin from
the last week, but they would throw in the ones they
planned on committing after service ended! Is it any
wonder people continue in sin when we insist they basically declare it (and therefore, define themselves by it) on
a regular basis? I only compare myself in this sense to one
other Christian—and that's the old me, before the grace
conversion. And the sin/repent/lather/rinse/repeat cycle
only led to disappointment, frustration, and eventually
burnout. The joy, the purity, even the good works themselves, are all far more prominent since I stopped trying
to constantly confess every area I used to view as a weak
spot and started declaring and practicing the truth that,
through Jesus, #iamholy.

"But my Bible says, 'Confess your sins to one another.'"
It sure does. Did you notice it also immediately follows
that up with, "Pray for each other so you may be healed?"
Wouldn't you agree that's a pretty clear declaration that
the sin you just confessed needs to be healed...not confessed again the next day, and the next day, on and on, forever? Once you realize that through Jesus you are already

holy in the sight of God and start walking out truth, accountability stops being another painful, embarrassing, or empty religious exercise. It's actually fun to have a brother, sister, mother, or father in the faith that reminds you who you actually *are* on a regular basis.

It's possible to start believing and living according to lies at any point in our faith journey. The confession to God and each other, however, needs to be from a place of knowing you're already a good tree from the moment you deny yourself and follow Jesus! You tell me which seems more effective:

- *Traditional accountability*: "I just need to confess some sin. I know the Bible says to honor authority, but I've been consumed by hateful and bitter thoughts against my boss for months now. I just feel defeated, and would love if you could join me in prayer that I make it through each day without cussing him out. That really wouldn't sit well with the one other person in the office who knows I go to church. At least I can console myself that everyone at work has to know that Christians aren't perfect…just forgiven."

- *Accountability from the #iamholy perspective*: "Hey, man, I know I laid down the right to hold unforgiveness against my boss when I started following Jesus. Through grace I am being transformed into His image, but I confess I've been believing and acting according to the old lies lately. Can you join me in praying that God fills me with a fresh revelation of His love as I seek Him this week? Let's just begin to thank Him for the grace to love that guy. Also, I'm going to meditate on the truth that God forgave me for some pretty serious stuff so that I could forgive others like my boss...for what now seems pretty mild. Do you think you could text me a couple of times a week to encourage me in that?"

That does seem like it would be more effective. But if I don't confess my sins—at least to God—every day, doesn't that mean I'm pretending to be perfect and living in denial?

No, it means you're making the Answer your focus and beginning to manifest Him instead of those old issues. Focusing on the way we word things can quickly get lame, but I don't think it's a stretch to shift from "Lord, I'm so wicked, please make me holy" to "Lord, open my eyes to the truth that *I am holy* in Christ and help me access the grace to manifest You today!" I know most of you are pounding the table at this point, begging for some profound theological concepts. You're in luck.

THEOLOGY TIME (I'M A YOUTH PASTOR, CAN I CONTINUE WITHOUT EVERYONE CHECKING THEIR SMARTPHONES? THANKS.)

There are two types of righteousness: imputed and imparted. Both are free gifts of grace received by faith. Imputed righteousness means Christ became our sin so that, in Him, we have become the very holiness of God. Derek Levendusky explains, "This verse (2 Corinthians 5:21—we discuss it in depth in Chapter 3, but for now please feel free to look it up) teaches that all the righteousness in Christ's bank account was transferred to yours, and therefore, through

Christ, our sins are wiped away and we are now as righteous as Jesus in the eyes of God the Father."[2] This is *justification*. It means as long as we repent, we have fully holy and right standing with God regardless of our past performance because we have put our faith in what Christ already accomplished in His death and resurrection.

Imparted righteousness refers to *sanctification*. This is certainly what people mean when they talk about Christianity being a "lifelong process." This process of maturity occurs each day as we face tests and trials. The difference through the eyes of a grace conversion is that this is not a daily grind, but instead, part of the good news! It means today I will look even more like Jesus than I did yesterday. I will be more patient, more joyful, more loving, and all kinds of other fun demonstrations of Christ in me.

What I want to get across (and have rarely heard taught) is that there is *no hope for effective long term sanctification without the revelation that Jesus already provided full justification.* Unless our consistently improving character comes from a place of already knowing my position before God is #iamholy—because of His finished work on the Cross—it has become "works" and won't last.

OK, great depth there, Mr. Didactic Christology. Can we get practical again?

Who keeps letting this guy in here? But I was heading in that direction anyway. Why will I look more like Jesus tomorrow than today? Simply because I have had one more day to *pray* and one more day to *practice*. Let's elaborate on those two concepts:

Pray

We get before God in a place of intimacy, pour out our heart to Him, and receive as He pours His grace into us. If we acknowledge He is an all-knowing God, then we have to admit He knows everything that will test us that day and can release in advance the grace, love, and forgiveness we need. We open the Word of God and declare the truth within that speaks to the person He created each of us to be. We praise and worship Him because He is worthy and He loved us first, regardless of whether we feel like it or how "good" or "bad" the day is going so far.

Let's do everyone a favor, friend, and not waste any time doing the classic evangelical disclaimer, "We're not being religious here, no pressure if you miss a day, yada yada" as I make this next statement. I don't want to "miss a day!" What is more important than time with Jesus? Sorry if some people have turned it into legalism, pressure, manipulation, empty religious discipline, or dead works...but that doesn't change what the truth says.

Here goes: We need to follow Christ's example in both "praying without ceasing" and "withdrawing to lonely places to pray." We want to get to a place where we constantly have our hearts turned to the Holy Spirit; just as important is a regular, separated, devotional time. (Spoiler alert: Chapter 5 covers this in detail.)

Practice

Every time a situation comes up that would have led us to sin or misplaced focus in the past, we can access the grace provided through Christ in us. We now believe and then act upon the truth that #iamholy. We proclaim that we were forgiven to forgive, and we release anyone who wrongs us. We believe the declarations in God's Word louder than the circumstances of life. What someone says or does (or fails to say or do) throughout the course of our day has no effect on our joy or on our kingdom purposes for those moments as we believe, declare, and live by the promises He has given us.

"Give me some examples of these promises!" OK, OK…calm down, tiger. Here are some good ones: The joy of the Lord is my strength. I am accepted by God. I have lost my life to find it in Him. (That means I laid down the rights that were only mine because I was born into the sinful nature. "Rights" such as unforgiveness, unrighteous anger, and insecurity—all of these have been crucified with Christ and no longer live in me.) My God meets all my needs according to His glorious riches in Christ Jesus.

As we begin to move from head knowledge of the Bible to taking hold of these promises, His truth begins speaking louder than anything life throws at us. Now the process of maturity looks different than it used to. It's no longer a struggle. We begin to understand what living "victory to victory" looks like *whether or not circumstances are 100 percent pleasant.* When my friend says something insulting, instead of wasting time being hurt or withdrawing from the relationship, I immediately allow Christ in me to release forgiveness. When my kids forget how amazing they are and act obnoxious, I let His grace rise up in me and discipline them from a place of love instead of frustration and impatience. When I lose my job, instead of falling apart and whining to God about how it's not fair because I've always been faithful to tithe, I thank Him that He is my provider and begin to use the extra time for His glory as I expectantly pray about the next season of life. Are we starting to notice the difference? One is the way the world trained us to react—which up until now we've justified by calling it "natural." The other way is responding to the leading of the Holy Spirit.

Practice isn't "works." It's grace.

Want the most extreme real-life example I have of the "practice" aspect? The knock at my door at 4:30 a.m. where a police officer informs me that my thirty-two-year-old brother John (which means "loved by God." Wow!) had suffered a horrific motorcycle accident in his home state. I soon find out from a phone conversation with the head surgeon that John had flatlined twice in the first few hours. Yes, my brother had died—not once but twice—and had to be brought back. We should prepare for the likelihood he will exist either as a vegetable from the brain injury, or paralyzed from the spinal injury. A plethora of other physical issues exist as well.

Now how does one respond to this news? I could do it the old way: cry, shake my fist, moan about how young he is, call around for "prayer" (religious code for "sympathy"), spend the day—and the whole time my brother is in medical limbo—asking God, "Why?" and, "Didn't I pray a hedge of protection around him? How can a good God allow this? I thought You loved me!"

Or through His grace in me, I can practice the #iamholy way: I laid down the right to take God to court and question His goodness when I began following Him. My response now looks like this: Get on my knees and thank the Lord that He is always good. Begin to declare over my brother truth from the Word of God that He is faithful to finish what He starts. I know John isn't finished yet because he has had promises prayed over him that have yet to be fulfilled. Agree that the physical healing Jesus provided on the Cross will begin to manifest in my brother's brain, back, ribs, and entire body. Bow before my Savior King and declare, similar to Shadrach and the fellas in their fiery furnace: "No matter how this turns out, You are

God and You are good. But I hold strong to Your promise that You have healed John, and I thank You for Your love." I still call around for prayer, but I put forth the request based on the Answer and not fear or panic.

This seems like a good place for a brief reminder: no condemnation. This is a place in the Spirit that we continually pursue. I haven't "arrived." If the last crisis you faced led to a response that looked like the old way described above, I cannot stress strongly enough to you that I once—several years after becoming a Christian—reacted that exact way to *getting a speeding ticket*. But as we recognize the truth that "it is finished" in Christ (again, the best description I can come up with as to how we most effectively get on this path is "prayer and practice") we get closer every day to the #iamholy way.

See, I had officially crossed the line into grace that last October. I had been preaching it in the youth ministry since early December. Every week we focused on the finished work of Christ which manifests in our life in several ways…one of the most obvious being that we begin to believe truth louder than circumstances. And this motorcycle accident happened at the end of January. To say the rubber had met the road was literally and metaphorically true.

Two of my spiritual sons from the Rising were coming over that very night for a regularly scheduled time of hanging out and studying the Word. They called me a few hours before, certain it would be postponed as they had heard about the accident. I wondered out loud why we would cancel. They had no response as the "wisdom" of the world had been intentionally dismissed from our gatherings months earlier. We met as planned.

We had built the kind of trust where honesty was the only policy. One hour into our time, I had to ask. Besides the obvious physical tiredness, was I any different—spiritually, mentally, emotionally—than I had been two nights earlier when all was well and I stood before them and their peers to preach believing God's Word louder than any of life's unpleasant situations? They shook their heads, in awe of His unfathomable grace. "Pastor Mike, you are exactly the same."

As my family, friends, and extended Christian family around the world prayed from a place of victory, miracles began to happen almost immediately. Everything negative the medical staff was "certain" they would find based on the external symptoms simply wasn't there when they took another look. Paralysis, having to remove a chunk of his skull due to brain swelling, ruptured internal organs—all initial diagnoses that were proven incorrect upon a second examination. We told the doctor repeatedly these miracles occurred through the hand of God. He resisted this explanation but finally admitted, "I have never seen a recovery like this. It's absolutely remarkable."

I am convinced that God poured out an extra "dose" of grace to carry me through that time. But the capacity to receive and walk in it after hearing one of the worst pieces of news I could imagine had been built up over months of practicing believing His promises louder than the less extreme tests and trials of life. Let's decide in our hearts to make a commitment to "pray and practice" every day.

"I'LL NEVER DO THIS SIN AGAIN. I KNOW I'VE SAID IT EVERY WEEK FOR THE LAST EIGHT YEARS, BUT I MEAN IT THIS TIME, LORD!"

I am completely justified, I am being sanctified... #iamholy! But I am not talking about claiming to have achieved a practice of sinless perfection. Our friend Job learned the folly of trying that, am I right? I just want to ask, has a focus on the fact that we will always have the capacity or the ability to sin ever led to *anything* other than more sin? For years we have tried really hard not to sin. I question the fruit of these efforts. Would you agree it seems oftentimes that at best, we have merely produced somewhat effective sin management? Swearing less than the guy in the cubicle next to me, not allowing the anger from that morning at home to show itself during worship at church, making sure our gossip is limited to "what I would say to their face anyway," only being unfaithful in our thoughts...I'll stop now. Remember, no condemnation! I only present an opportunity to let the Lord lead us into a more excellent way. What if instead of entering each day—or each moment—trying to avoid things that have been weak spots in the past, we change our focus?

Did you know the subconscious mind fails to recognize negatives? That is, if you meditate on a thought such as "I will not sin," you do not internally recognize the "not," and you are in effect saying, "I will sin."

You can fill in the blank with "blatant" sins such as lying, drug abuse, or gossip—or mind-sets such as depression, worry, or bitterness. Let's use the example of something I struggled with for years after salvation: speaking damaging words to others.

Each day after prayer or studying Scripture on the subject, my mind would say, "I hope I don't use my words destructively today. I'm going to try really hard. Harder than yesterday, I promise! In fact, Lord, I want to make a covenant in Your presence so You can keep me accountable in this. I vow that I will only use my words to encourage today!"

I would succeed for a few days, weeks, or most likely, hours. Then, when somebody did something offensive to me and I responded with what was "natural" (harsh words), now I'm into multiple levels of condemnation. First, I have broken the command in Ephesians to use words to build up, not tear down. Also, to have done so, I obviously didn't "take every thought captive." Strike two. Add to that, as I have committed the very sin I vowed not to that morning...*I have lied to God!* How can I ever see myself as holy again?

I'm telling you through experience that when you start the day (or even a moment of temptation) declaring instead, "Thank You, Lord, that Christ lives in me, that You created me to be a good son, that because through Him I am holy. I'm excited for the grace to use my words to encourage people today," guess what? You are far more likely to manifest that!

Most would contend that trying not to sin is a good thing. I agree, in the sense that it usually comes from a rightly motivated heart. That is, Christians who want to become more like Jesus. But after fifteen years of living this way and producing disciples in ministry that operated similarly, I am now convinced it is a form of Christian slavery.

Christian slavery?

Think about it. Maybe some of you can relate to my story. I was raised in a Christian home and was a pretty good kid...until I hit six years old. The crime sprees, the thirty-six-hour drug binges, the nonstop jaywalking; first grade was a tough go-round. (There's my entry in the next "my testimony is way more powerful than yours" contest that occasionally occurs in charismatic church gatherings.) But in reality, I was a slave to sin for years. I could stop temporarily with willpower, but long-term I was powerless to change those things that I hated about myself. A resolution might last hours, days, or even weeks…but I could never be truly free in my own strength. Then, at eighteen years old, God radically saved me. He healed my heart and supernaturally set me free from the bondage to my sins.

My soul burned with passion and gratitude. I told everyone I knew—I don't think it's a stretch to say almost two hundred fellow high school students heard me share my faith over those last three months of senior year. I even went to Christian college to train as a youth pastor, because maybe there could be some redemption for the years I wasted. But over time, something else happened.

The movie *Amistad* portrays part of the story of early American slavery. An early scene that took place on the boat ride across the ocean really struck a chord with me. After many torturous days at sea with heavy chains around their necks, the slaves rise up and overcome their captors. I rejoiced in my seat with them as they threw off their shackles and shouted for joy as they tasted long-awaited freedom! As they excitedly celebrate, the background music soon turns ominous. A second boat full of reinforcements shows up and shortly after experiencing the sheer elation of liberty, new, equally heavy chains are placed around their necks.

I remember thinking to myself that had to be one of the lowest emotions humanly possible to experience. The sweetness of exchanging slavery for freedom brutally snatched away and replaced with more slavery in a matter of minutes. What could be worse?

I feel like that's exactly what happened to me spiritually. Jesus set me free from my bondage to all the blatant sins that went with the partying lifestyle. And less than a year later, I had found a whole new set of chains.

I was a slave to people's expectations of what a good Christian life should look like. I was in bondage to my circumstances. I knew so many biblical principles like "the joy of the Lord is my strength," but when life brought tests and trials, joy was nowhere to be found. Bad situations equaled a bad day. The chains of the former sins were gone forever, but they were exchanged for mind-sets such as discouragement and unbelief.

This continued for fifteen years. At one point I had a thriving youth ministry. As long as each gathering went well, I was doing great in my "call." But I got further and further away from my first love. At eighteen years old, the Father had spoken into me. When I turned my heart to Him at my lowest point, He simply said, "You're My son. Welcome home, all is forgiven." That's how He captured my heart.

As the months went on, that passion began to turn to "maturity." Instead of simply drawing closer to Him and sharing the good news of His love with others, I learned that a life surrendered to Jesus should look a certain way. It doesn't matter how long we've been born again—actually, it often seems it's because of the distance between our current mind-set and that early revelation of "first-love"—at any point in our faith journey we can start believing lies.

And I did—I thought being a successful follower of Jesus defined itself by results in my life and ministry. I became an expert at doing better through willpower. Looking back, it was a masterful performance. And how could I teach something I didn't really know myself? We reproduce disciples after our own kind. Many times over those fifteen years I asked God how the teens in my ministry could have such powerful gatherings—marked by His presence, repentance for sin, and sincere vows to do better—and still go out and be dominated by life's circumstances and what other people thought about them. I was thrilled that because of His grace we could have a great time in God. But I knew we were still having a terrible time in life. There had to be a better way.

Maybe some of us can relate—we've been part of an awesome service with passionate worship, a memorable altar experience, or a preached message that seemed straight from the Lord's heart to ours. And yet two days later when life brought trials we were right back to asking, "God, where are You? I thought that feeling was real but it just didn't last!" Maybe some of us have even looked at our lives and wondered why it seemed no different than the life of someone who doesn't profess to be a Christian. What then does true freedom look like?

I AM FREE

> Let me be clear, the Anointed One has set us free— not partially, but completely and wonderfully free! We must always cherish this truth and stubbornly refuse to go back into the bondage of our past!
> —GALATIANS 5:1, TPT

Ah, there it is. Jesus has set us completely free! If you've never seen *The Dark Knight Rises*, I'll pray for you. But you also may want to skip this next paragraph. When Bruce is at the bottom of the insurmountable pit, he attaches the safety cord to himself and starts the awe-inspiring climb to freedom. But he fails every time. He can't quite make the leap from the pit to a new life above ground. He sincerely and wholeheartedly wants to make the change, but something is holding him back. *Only when he totally removes the safety cord—which, in essence, prophetically declares that he is completely and wonderfully free from every tie to the prison—does he successfully leave his bondage in the past and enter into true freedom.*

How does this relate to our God-given supernatural freeing from those things that lead to death? We've talked at length about the importance of cherishing truth...now how do we go about refusing to back into bondage to sin?

Justin Kendrick has amazing insight into this area of slavery vs. freedom. Specifically, the deception that many of us have bought into—especially as Americans—that "freedom" means freedom *from* religion, the mind-set of "I'm not accountable to anyone, and I can do what I want." The reality? No, I can't.[3]

That kind of counterfeit freedom actually puts us in bondage to the things we thought demonstrated our liberty. For instance: the freedom to eat whatever I want. *"Can't nobody tell me to eat vegetables. I'm free to eat candy 24/7."* Well, maybe for a few weeks when you're fourteen years old, but eventually what you put in your body will cause it to break down in a bad way. It will get to the point where it cannot function or process as it was designed to. Food, or anything else pursued to its fullest extent, will end up making us physically sick. What about the freedom to pursue multiple romantic partners? Setting aside the ever-increasing odds of bodily affliction as a result of the sexual connections, we've seen person after person have their hearts ripped apart by break-ups, unfaithfulness, and consistently broken relationships. So many will carry around scars from this that negatively affect every relational area of their lives, forever.

True freedom, says Kendrick, is not "nobody telling me what to do," but the freedom to be married to a perfect, holy, loving Being. "The highest form of human freedom is slavery to God. That is, the more bound I am to the One who is ultimately good, the more free I actually become!"[4] Only in that joining together will we find true freedom.

Here's why: Because when we willingly offer ourselves as love slaves to He who is love personified, *we finally settle the issue* that He is always good. No matter what circumstances come our way, we are free of questioning His goodness. My pastor, mother, or accountability brother no longer has to twist my arm to pray or seek His face. I wholeheartedly want Him alone and desire that His kingdom come and His will be done in and through me.

No more will we live trying not to go to hell, or trying not to fall into this sin or that sin. Creation has been longing for sons and daughters of God to be revealed. Here we are! Cities will be transformed as we rise up having willingly laid down our own lives to be joined to Him, declaring #iamholy as a city on the hill, a lamp on a stand![5]

So what makes a man or woman willing to embrace true freedom and live as holy slaves to righteousness? If it's not willpower, striving, or Bible knowledge, where does it come from?

As with almost every important question in life, the answer comes down to Heart lyrics: What about love?

Chapter 2

I AM LOVED

On our darkest day God did not lose sight
of us, in our most rebellious moment God
said, "That's not you, I know who you are!"

—Dan Mohler[1]

It was the unconditional nature of God's
love that most captivated the heart of the
apostle Paul and that should captivate ours.

—Paul Washer[2]

I n most Christian circles, "God loves you" is obvious
statement number one. You learn it around the time
you learn to breathe. Growing up in church, the first
song I ever learned was the Alphabet Song. (How did they
make it rhyme like that? P...V...Z—just brilliant!) The
second song I ever learned, naturally: Jesus Loves Me.

(The third, for those of you who are wondering:
"Coming to America" by Neil Diamond. That song is so
good, he can rhyme "free" with "dream" and it still rocks!)

You could ask a million evangelical Christians if God
loves them. And all of them would answer, in some
fashion: "Yes, of course God loves me. What sort of silly
question is that?"

We concluded last chapter that willpower, resolution,
and even the best of motives won't lead to true and consistent holiness. I submit that the *only* thing that will cause
us to live #iamholy is the love of God. And yet, we just

established that virtually everyone knows the concept is true. It's safe to say this knowledge hasn't yet led to the consistent freedom and righteousness we long for.

Could it be that understanding of a fact is not the same as an encounter with the reality of that truth? Someone could explain to me that skydiving is exhilarating. I can mull that statement over, decide it makes sense, and begin living with that mental acknowledgement. Any time someone asked me what skydiving was like, I would explain that it's fun. We could even start a church that sings a few songs about that truth every Sunday.

But when I actually jam my body into a plane slightly bigger than my couch, fly 14,000 feet off the ground, lean out of where the door should be (but isn't), and jump out for a full minute of glorious free-fall...I *am forever impacted by the revelation* of "Wow...this is exhilarating!"

I'm not talking about making feelings our guide. I'm talking about a real heart encounter with the Father's love vs. an intellectual notation that God cares about us. Remember how it comes—through prayer and practice. When we read the Bible as a love letter from heaven to me personally, when we get before God every day regardless of our current emotional state and simply ask to be filled with more of His love, when we practice living focused on Christ crucified no matter what situations life brings our way—*something starts to change.*

UNCONDITIONAL LOVE

A line gets crossed when we catch the revelation that the Lord really, really loves us. The Bible calls it "first love." Maybe you prefer "anyway love." He loved us first. He loved us when we lived as His enemies. I'm not saying

He loved everything we thought, said, or did, but the Word makes it clear the way He viewed *us* never changed through any of that. I may have been rebellious, bitter, and mean-spirited in my behavior, but He didn't define me by those things. He still saw me as a lost son and longed to be gloriously united in relationship. If every bit of His punishment was poured out on Jesus at the Cross, what was left for me? Mercy. Forgiveness, grace, patience, compassion. Love!

Yes, my actions had consequences. Every sin invited death into my body and soul. But no matter what I did or where I went, it didn't change my Father's heart toward me. Do we really understand there are no conditions on God's love? That's the revelation that wins hearts and turns people's lives away from sin and death and toward laying down everything to follow Him.

Romans 6:15 states: "For sin shall no longer be your master, because you are not under law, but under grace." Is it reasonable to imply that if we are trying to obey (as one under the law) through willpower, that sin can certainly master us? It's safe to say I'm not the only one who lived that experience. But once we encounter that outpouring of God's unconditional love, that wonderful grace conversion...that's when sin truly and finally shall not be our master! My friend Leahcim prefers equations over sentences. Here you go, buddy: God's gift of grace through Jesus + me believing that truth = #iamholy.

First Timothy 1:12–14, TPT goes even further:

> My heart spills over with thanks to God for the way
> He continually empowers me, and our Lord Jesus,
> the Anointed One, who found me trustworthy
> and who authorized me to be His partner in this

ministry. Mercy kissed me, even though I used to be a blasphemer, a persecutor of believers, and a scorner of what turned out to be true. God knew that I was ignorant and didn't know what I was doing. I was flooded with such incredible grace, like a river overflowing its banks, until I was full of faith and love for Jesus, the Anointed One!

I tried my best to be full of faith and love? No—*I was flooded with such incredible grace*...until *I was full of faith and love for Jesus*. I love the description of how when Paul (and each of us) was in the middle of manifesting all that nasty sin, "Mercy kissed me!" God knew we were ignorant; He never changes, and I seem to remember Jesus saying "forgive them Father; they know not what they do." What's the only thing that shows us we're wrong (and at the exact same time, gives us the power to finally change)? The unconditional firstlove of God!

Oh, How I Love Jesus ... Because He First Loved Me

A declaration of Psalm 116:1–6 has led our youth ministry family into worship many times. Let's note several things it doesn't say: I love the Lord...because it's the right thing to do. I love the Lord...because my mom said I'm a Christian. I love the Lord...because I prayed a prayer I barely remember years ago asking Jesus "into my heart." I love the Lord...because I mentally acknowledge His death and resurrection.

It says: I love the Lord...for He heard my voice! He heard my cry for mercy! Because He turned His ear to me, I will call on Him as long as I live! The cords of death entangled me, the anguish of the grave came upon me; I was overcome by trouble and sorrow. Then I called on the name of the Lord: O Lord, save me! The Lord is gracious and righteous; our God is full of compassion!

Would you say that's a little better than "Who's ready to worship, dudes?" As we declare the truth that He sought us, He called to us, He saved us from trouble and sorrow, *He loved us*, our hearts respond with gratitude and praise, and worship begins to rise!

I can't live #iamholy or ask anyone else to do the same until this truth takes root: God seems to think you living is worth Jesus dying.[3] He shed His blood for me and for you. Yes, you reading the book right now! I pray even at this very moment you would receive the overwhelming thought that as they pressed the thorns into His forehead, as they spit in His face, as they drove the spikes through His wrists... *He was thinking about being united with you.*

He rescued me from addiction, shame, fear, frustration—and it was done even as He knew I would ignore and reject Him for years. This is #firstlove. This is the kindness of God that leads us to repentance.

It's all over the Bible. We mentioned 1 John 3 in the introduction. The majority of that chapter goes into detail on how if we are in Christ, we cannot keep on sinning. If Jesus lives in us, we will love our brothers and sisters. It's no surprise that the very first verse in the chapter about living holy is "How great is the love the Father has lavished on us, that we should be called children of God! And that is what we are!" The "no longer practicing sin" part will only flow from our lives if we get a hold of the "God forever lavishes His love on me no matter how I've behaved because I'm His son or daughter" part! Once I repent, #iamholy already in my heavenly Father's eyes because of what Jesus did. But there's more! Sanctification—the process of maturity—stops being stressful and starts being a joy as I submit to Him daily, motivated only by the love He pours out on me constantly.

TRUE REPENTANCE

I think if we take a look at our typical prayer times up to this point, many of us spend a ton of time crying or confessing or focusing on all the ways we have fallen short of "Christian perfection." Why don't we instead try just letting Him love us? My grace conversion began when a spiritual mother challenged me to stop "praying good" and take a season just to ask God to reveal how He really saw me. It changed me forever. (To be clear, even though it's biblical and has happened to several trustworthy people I know, I have not personally heard God speak out loud. These are all things best described as a sense of what was being spoken to my heart).

It started with, "You're my son, and I love you." It continued with, "You're my son, and I love you." Then, He went into much of what I believed about myself…bad, neutral, and even "good" (backhanded compliments, really) that people had spoken over me. I'll never forget the time He said, "What they said about you wasn't true, son. I created you, and I know you. You're faithful and true, and I love your humility." Come on, never again will somebody's misguided criticism of my character affect me *one iota*. My Father has burned in my heart the actual truth.

DEPARTMENT OF CORRECTIONS

I can already hear the "discernment ministries" firing up a barrage of blog posts about how that's a statement from someone who considers himself above correction. Let's be proactive here: There's a place for true biblical correction. I embrace it myself from spiritual fathers and mothers, brothers and sisters I'm in relationship with—and even (once) a person who really didn't care about me and whose own motives were suspect—because God used it to deal with an area where I was blindly believing a lie. I apply it, when necessary, to the young men and women my wife and I mentor.

However, effective correction *is* always *given in the context of who that person really is, and not allowing the problem behavior to change how we relate to them.* I'm not even talking about merely employing the classic "encourage, correct, encourage" technique, though there's wisdom in that. I mean, remind them who they really are—how God sees them and how you've seen them manifest that and grow in those areas. We earn the right to speak into someone's life by proving that we're sincerely for them. Ask questions to find out where their heart is at before pulling out any "one size fits all" discipline. Then, the correction can be Spirit-led, wise, and actually produce the result of accelerated sanctification.

It's the personal attacks (sometimes disguised as "loving" correction) that don't affect me anymore. God has already spoken to the man He created me to be, loves ferociously, and couldn't be prouder of. If anyone thinks their opinion (usually colored by their own toxic experiences) is going to cause me to doubt what He says, good luck with that. People of all ages are starting to get excited about life on that side of grace. A Dan Mohler concept has become a running joke at the Rising. If anyone wants to try to emotionally abuse us, the result is probably going to be they themselves feeling emotionally abused by the utter fruitlessness of their efforts. *"You're a jerk."* "Well, God doesn't seem to think so." *"You're ugly."* "Nah, He says there's no flaw in me." *"Man, nothing I say can make this guy react negatively! I need some counseling."*

This is the place where "If God is for me, who can be against me" becomes a joyful reality, and not just a nice Bible verse to quote. I am loved!

TRUE REPENTANCE, CONTINUED

Why does repentance have to be a long, drawn-out, teary process? Listen, friends, these are confessions of a former, um, confession addict! I thought I needed to demonstrate how sorry I really felt to prove my sincerity to God. King David refused all food and entertainment as he kept his face pressed into the floor for a week. Now that's repentance, I thought! The truth is, though we certainly should move in that same spirit of humility and godly fear before the King of kings, David's episode took place before Jesus finished the work of His death and resurrection. Times have changed! We can now approach the throne of grace with confidence. Why would we waste that sort of time punishing ourselves when we could be letting His kindness lead us to repent and return to His will instantly— and start manifesting His glory again instead of moping around all brokenhearted?

I want to make clear I am not talking about being flippant. Anyone can certainly offer up a weak "sorry, God" while planning to continue in willful sin. That's a bad idea.

I mean I am pursuing a place in my walk of faith that looks like this: When I do step out of grace and believe a lie, *in the moment that the Holy Spirit convicts me, I respond by repenting and turning my heart back to God in a matter of seconds.* It's sincere, pure, and I don't waste any extra time outside of His will, accomplishing nothing of worth for eternity. Only His love can provide such a supernatural acceleration!

Allow me to paraphrase how one fourteen-year-old young man explained this concept as it related to his corporate worship experience at the Rising. "Man, it's like I used to spend the whole 'worship' time feeling bad for not being good enough—either sins from that week, or being afraid to share my faith at school, or even trying to make myself feel like worshipping in the moment and failing. But now (since we started focusing on grace through the finished work of Jesus), worship is awesome! I don't have to spend twenty minutes 'repenting,' I just get to spend time honoring and connecting with my Dad who loves me!"

WHY GRACE WORKS

I believe the biggest reason we cling to the "we're all going to sin, but maybe if you pray and read the Bible a lot you'll try hard not to do it too much" teachings—in church and especially youth ministry—is that we are afraid that imparting the freedom we actually have in Christ will lead to rebellion or debauchery in the name of "grace."

"Pastor Mike said we don't have to try to improve our behavior anymore. Forget you, Mom!" (Throws chair through window.)

I would venture a guess that the Word has something to say about that:

> "Beloved ones, God has called us to live a life of freedom in the Holy Spirit. But don't view this wonderful freedom as an opportunity to set up a base of operations in the natural realm. Freedom means that we become so completely free of

self-indulgence that we become servants of one another, expressing love in all we do."

—GALATIANS 5:13, TPT

Freedom comes from choosing to be a slave to God. We make that choice when His love overtakes our heart. Once we lay down our lives and follow Him, we have complete freedom in the Holy Spirit. That intimacy with God is so much more amazing than the temporary pleasure of self-indulgent sin. Of course we will choose to serve and express love!

Derek Levendusky's book *Discipleship by Grace* became a huge catalyst in my own awakening during that sweet year of being changed forever by the love of Jesus. He provides a great description of how our newfound freedom will lead not to abuse, but to more love:

> Built into grace is the instruction for holiness because grace alters our desires and purifies our motives. Grace actually causes us to choose what is good and right.[4]

He goes on to compare it to his love for his children:

> Now, down in the county courthouse, there are probably scores of laws in the law books about what I can't do to my children. Even so, not once have I had to go down to the courthouse to study the laws so I can figure out how to properly parent my children. Love has already taught me that. Because I love my children, I fulfill all the laws written in the law books.[5]

When Jesus says in John 14:21 That those who love Him obey His commands, Derek's (and mine...and almost every Christian I've ever encountered) response for years was, "Whoa! I better obey Him to prove that I love Him!" But we now see that "Jesus was not teaching obedience as a *condition* of our love, but as a *result* of our love."[6]

We have come to describe this as the "want to." When we let God continually fill us to overflowing with His love and grace, we supernaturally want to think, speak, and act differently. I remember the eighth grader in my youth ministry who—after years of attending church with his family (and around half a dozen times praying the "sinner's prayer" through the years)—decided to finally put his faith in Jesus at one of our gatherings. He didn't "feel" anything like many did at the altar, but he took hold of the truth that God did, had always, and would always, radically love him. Two weeks later, he had one question for me: "Why am I so nice now?"

The answer: the captivating love of Jesus overtook his heart. Quality religious instruction, good Christian parents, even noble motives didn't make him "want to" live holy. Only the consuming revelation of God's grace and passion burning inside led to a consistent change in word, thought, and behavior.

There's a thirteen-year-old young woman who sat under this kind of #iamholy (grace, what Jesus already accomplished, mind-blowing love of God, our created value) teaching for several months at the Rising. Quiet by nature, her mom suggested I ask her to sing at our annual Open Mic night. I did, and she reluctantly agreed. We were excited when she said she'd be singing an original song she had recently written. We had no idea she was about to blow the roof off of the place. She began to play the piano, and as an appreciation for her hidden talent mixed with reverence for the unconditional love of the Father swept the room, she sang:

> Well, You told me I was imperfect
> Then You said to me I was worth it
> You picked me up and placed me on my feet
> And You said to me: "you're My masterpiece"
>
> And now I'm not afraid
> God it's everything You say is true
> And now that I have faith
> Everything I do will be for You
> And when I fall down
> You'll pick me up and put me on my feet
> You will say to me: "you're My masterpiece"
>
> Everything I say, everything I do
> Every day I live this life it will be for You
> I used to think You weren't pleased
> But now I am free to be me
> You are my Creator, I am Your masterpiece
>
> —"Your Masterpiece,"
> Rea Summer Steyne, 2013

Excuse me for a second, I think my wife is chopping onions in the other room (wipes eyes). Something happens when we go from knowing the Bible says "for God so loved the world" to walking with the revelation that He ferociously loves *me personally*. He created us to reveal His glory, He loved us no matter what we did or where we went, and—once we repent and accept His free gift—when we do fall down, He picks us up and reminds us who we *are*...His masterpiece.

Only once we begin to grasp this can we honestly say, "Every day I live this life, it will be for You." Only when we are captivated by His love can we approach the throne of grace with confidence. Let's stop wasting time with counterfeit repentance, spend time every day simply letting Him love us, and every day will become an adventure where it's natural to stand up and boldly declare with our lives: "I am holy!"

Chapter 3
I AM LOVING

No one has seen God at any time; if we
love one another, God abides in us, and
His love is perfected in us. By this we
know that we abide in Him and He in us,
because He has given us of His Spirit.

—1 JOHN 4:12–13, NASB

CAN YOU FEEL THE LOVE TONIGHT

WHY DOES GOD love us? How come He forgives us? I don't mean "He forgives us because He loves us, and He loves us…um, because He loves us." I'm pretty thrilled His love and forgiveness defy my logic. I mean *why* does He love and forgive us—as in, what do we do with that revelation? What is the only possible response we can have to such mind-blowing grace?

The answer is that we become those things to the people around us. We see it all over the Bible: Forgive, as I have forgiven. Be holy, as I am holy. Be merciful, for you have been shown mercy. We've discussed the fact that none of this is ultimately sustainable in our lives through willpower alone. We must be captivated by His love daily and get before Him as He pours out every last drop of grace that we need.

I've heard a teaching that says we need to be getting filled up by God's love to replace what we're pouring out.

That seems like a good idea but can quickly turn into an excuse not to minister if we're "empty" or "drained." I'm talking about the next level. That is, living in a constant flow of His love *so that no matter how much we pour out, we remain full to overflowing.* Think of it as a cup sitting on a saucer. If you constantly pour your "cup" out to minister to others, you will in fact have to go back to God to get a refill. But if your cup is continually overflowing, anyone will be able to "drink out of the saucer" and refresh themselves without putting any drain on your own Source.[1] See, we *cannot* truly love unless we know His firstlove. That's why the "I am loved" comes first. As His love pours into us and overflows out of us, love naturally results.

First John 4 goes on to say whoever "knows not love"— that is, whoever is not living out Christ's love to the people around them—doesn't know God. Is that condemnation? *Well, you keep quoting the verse that says there's no condemnation in Christ, so...no?*

You get a gold star...or a Go-Gurt, whichever you prefer. I'd say John's statement becomes more of a way to measure where we are currently at in our intimate knowledge of God.

To paraphrase the legitimately great hip-hop theologian Timothy Brindle, "Jesus is Lord, your lips confess...but loving others is that confession's litmus test." (Timothy Brindle, "Fruit Inspection," from the Album Killing Sin, 2005, Lamp Mode Recordings)

THE RADICAL PERSPECTIVE OF 2 CORINTHIANS 5

In 2 Corinthians 5:14–21, Paul talks about the ministry of reconciliation. Basically, God reconciled—provided the way for people brought back into right relationship with

Him—through the finished work of Christ. Because of what Jesus did, anyone who simply turns their heart and puts their faith in His death as a propitiation for our sins— and His resurrection as the victory over them forever—*no longer has their sins counted against them.*

Jesus died, why? Because I'm a sinner constantly in need of a reminder how messed up I will be this side of heaven? No, "He died for *all,* that those who live *should no longer live for themselves but for Him* who died for them and was raised again" (2 Cor. 5:15)! That He loved me enough to die for me for the purpose of redeeming me; that He would delight to live in me and through me—it's overwhelming! It's staggering! It's the driving passion of my life to be woken up by His love every morning regardless of what I feel or don't feel, no matter if the circumstances that face me are pleasant or significantly less than pleasant! I get before Him and ask where He's staying that day and—whether I get specific direction or not—that love compels me to pour out the overflow on everyone I come in contact with.

How could I go back to focusing on myself, my "needs," when the Bible says I've been given every spiritual blessing in Christ? Everyone who's been around church longer than a year has heard Philippians 4:19 quoted. "God will meet all my needs according to His glorious riches in Christ Jesus." We can believe the principle behind this verse and still walk around needing affirmation from people, or we can start to live the truth declared here and stop putting expectations on people and start loving them! Think about it: If all my needs are met in Jesus, I will never leave a church badly. I will never whine about how Pastor So-and-So doesn't recognize my spiritual gift cluster. I will never get mad at my wife for being insensitive to my needs! How can I be disappointed or needy when God has promised that they are all met in Him?

He died in my place that I'm no longer lost, but found—restored to my created value as His son—so now I live for Him. I don't have to fake it, I don't have to work it up; all I have to do is stir up the gift that has already been placed within me. I encourage myself in the Holy Spirit, then I go out and live "Your kingdom come, Your will be done, on earth as it is in heaven." Does that sound better than "God, please help me make it through another day"? I love the thought from the preacher who said: "If life hands you lemons, just make lemonade...I don't think so! I don't feel like lemonade today. I want a Dr Pepper!"

There's a concept gaining momentum with this generation that flies in the face of youth ministry wisdom from the past. We've spent years being trained in trying to avoid being "in the red" (a business that is losing money). This is the "do our best to avoid major sin," "God, help me make it through today" teaching.

Young men and women of God are starting to rise up and live "in the black." This describes a company operating with a surplus! This surplus is the love and power of our living Savior. As we are filled to overflowing, it splashes on everyone around us. We need to put an end to living on the defensive. We named the Rising's pre-service prayer time after a powerful concept from a video game (this is where I usually make a Super Mario Brothers joke, but let's skip it today). It's called "Suppressive Fire." It's the picture of a soldier raining down so many bullets (a firestorm, if you will) that the enemy has to stay hidden and unable to strategize. Come on, that's good stuff right there. This is the place Jesus called us to when He spoke of violent prayer. We're not going to respond to another suicide at the local high school. We're going to invade that school with the love that has overtaken us and reach every student with the hope that God created them with an amazing destiny in Jesus!

Christ's love compels us. It drives us, it presses us, it is the fuel in our tank! If we are moved by anything other than the love of Jesus, we have fallen into a works mentality. Things that benefit society may result...but it's not sustainable.

My problem has always been that I actually have a lot of willpower. It makes me that much more likely to fall into works, and pride. I always knew living in a holy manner and doing ministry didn't earn salvation or even God's love. I knew that I lived that way because I loved Jesus. But any "success" I achieved in holiness or outreach depended on how I felt that day. I could go for a while and look pretty good, but eventually even I got tired of performing. It culminated in some serious burnout. Only when I got a hold of the truth that it was God's pleasure and will to predestine me as His son (Ephesians 1) did I start seeing consistent and long-lasting results in ministry. Only after the Holy Spirit showed me in the Word that #iamholy already through the finished work of Jesus did I start manifesting real holiness on a consistent basis. And only when He overwhelms me with His burning love every day can I press on toward the mark for the high prize of His calling! It's His love! Anything less is beating the air with our fists—accomplishing virtually nothing of eternal value.

And as Christ's love compels us, *we regard no one from a worldly point of view.* I had always been taught—and spent years teaching it myself—"Well, as Christians, we *have* to love everyone. But, of course, we're not going to *like* everyone!" That's the sin nature talking. What does that actually say? How do we love someone we don't like? Bite our lip and suppress our true feelings every time we're forced to spend time with them? *"Because of God's love, I just spent two hours at church sitting next to that guy whose personality I can't stand. I even smiled at him once! I'm a spiritual giant."* I think we can all admit that's what it has looked like up to this point.

One of the worst moments I experienced as a youth pastor happened during a pre-service student prayer one week in the early days of the Rising. Keep in mind, these were the "core" teens. One girl excitedly shared how she had invited her unchurched friend to that night's gathering and he had agreed to come. The girl two seats down from her immediately tensed up. "Uh oh," she began. "I don't like him very much. We actually got in a fight a few weeks ago and it's been all drama ever since."

Talk about quenching the Spirit! This group of committed prayer warriors immediately began debating the merits of this young man. Even those from other schools chose sides based on who they were better friends with out of the two girls involved. As this occurred well before my grace conversion, I can say my disappointment was palpable.

Everything worked out that night in the sense that our "no drama during the Rising gathering" policy ended up not being broken, but it was clear that we were still very much regarding people from a worldly point of view.

"GOD LOVES YOU, GOD LOVES ME, WE'RE A HAPPY FAMILY . . . AS LONG AS YOU DON'T OFFEND ME."

The Holy Spirit leads us into righteousness; it's only His love and kindness that permanently changes problem behaviors. The wisdom of this world trained us to "punish" people into changing by withdrawing when they act unpleasant. How many lives have surrendered to Jesus as a result of that "wisdom"? I count none, because that's not God's way! Our call to love is a call to like, too.

"How can I like them, Mike? You don't know what they did to me!" Maybe I don't, but God does and He's telling you to let it go and love them! Can we get to a place where we realize that not only does Jesus love us, but He likes us too? Why would He die the most painful death ever inflicted on one man for the end result of coming to live inside me if He didn't think I was worth spending every day with? He may not like every decision I made or every place I went, but *it never changed how He related to me as a person.* He never said, "I'm sick of you; come back when you're ready to act like a reasonable adult." How dare we presume to think or say what He never would! I'll say over and over again in this book: We will never be Jesus, but because He lives in and through us we can surrender to His way *every single time* and live like Him. In this example, let Christ in us lead us to love the formerly unlikable. Without pretending we enjoy a person's current behavior we can still honor the man or woman they have been created to be and relate to them accordingly!

Does this sound good, my brother in Christ? Does this sound unrealistic, woman of God? (I did that in case there is a couple like us where the wife likes to read over the husband's shoulder).

Keep reading, my friend(s). I used to think this was a pipe dream too, but it has become a consistent lifestyle for me and a growing number of others.

WHAT IS LOVE?

The Bible says no greater love exists than for a person to lay down their life for someone else. To paraphrase Miles McPherson: True love means wanting the best for the other person no matter what it costs you personally. And what is *always* truly best for everyone is the will of God.

How did we go from "I will lay down my life to see God's will fulfilled in yours" to "What have you done for me lately?" This applies to all interpersonal relations, but let's focus for a minute on the dating scene. Relationships for the teens I've observed through the years (and many adults, no?) are based on finding a significant other that meets *my* personal needs.

I love the way you make me feel. You make me a better person. Nothing in life compares to the way I feel when I'm with you. You make me feel... like a natural woman.

So when that guy tells that girl "I love you," what he is actually saying is, "I love *me*."

I love me so much, sweet thang. I'm so beautiful today. I'm the only one for me. I knock me off my feet, girl. Let me whisper sweet nothings in my ear. Me me me me me."

You can see it all over social media. Consider this real-life example from a youth we'll call Romeo (names changed—and spelling improved—to protect the overly sensitive and/or hormonal), posted on Facebook one sunny May 14:

> *I love Juliet Smith with all my heart. You've always been there for me, babe, and I'll never forget it. We'll be together until I die. I would do anything for you. Smooch!*

If that's not love, what is? Now consider his post on May 31:

I love Penelope Jones with all my heart. I love you so much it hurts, babe! Our parents may not understand, but you are my special one and only. My soul mate, my everything. We'll be together forever. Smooch!

And a little bit lower on the page:

Juliet Smith is scum and the world would be a better place without her in it.

Wow, what happened, Romeo? It stopped working for *me*. It's not you, it's *me*. She wasn't who *I* thought she was...*but me and Penelope, this is different.*

We all know so many Christians who have 1 Corinthians 13 posted somewhere in their house. We all know so few Christians who have it written on their hearts and manifest it daily. Love keeps no record of wrongs. It's only possible if we have tasted God's unconditional love and have started to embrace the truth that we were created to become it to the people around us!

Do we need to check our WWJD bracelets? I'll send you an "I AM HOLY" one if you want. On the night He was betrayed, Jesus broke bread and worshipped alongside the very brothers that did the betraying without one iota of bitterness. On the night we were betrayed, we slammed them on Twitter, called around to rally people to our celebration of victimhood, and months later when we were finally able to mention them in prayer, it sounded like: *"God, please change Jenny's heart so I can pray Your blessing on her. I know if I pray to bless her in her current gossipy state, and You answer that prayer, people will get the wrong idea and think that her behavior is OK because she's prospering. Just humble her, Lord, and fix all her ways that offend me, and then You'll really get the glory!"*

Come on, friends, I was there for years! Until I got the very clear sense what God was saying about this: Your part is just to bless them. Pray that I pour My love and grace upon them with no ulterior motive about them changing their behavior toward you.

LOOKING FOR LOVE IN ALL THE WRONG PLACES

We all know that because we were born into the sin nature we spend our pre-Christian days looking for love in all the wrong places, from impure sexual connections to unhealthy friendships, even changing our personality to fit in with people we don't actually care about that much to appease the beast called peer pressure.

The problem is that many of us "became Christians" by praying a prayer to include God in our stuff instead of laying down our lives to find them in Him. We actually continue to long for real love, and fill it with less than His best.

If we allow someone to hurt us, that longing we all have for love can be patched over with pity or sympathy from a friend. Misery loves company!

Nobody truly likes to be hurt, but we learn to cling to it because it's easy, familiar, and often earns us pity. The enemy and the wisdom of the world offer up so much counterfeit love to keep us from tasting and seeing that God is good. Pity is one of the most prominent examples. We think we show how good of a friend we are by patting someone on the shoulder and telling them we can't believe that this jerk treated them this way. "*There, there. It will be OK. He's not worth your tears.*"

How about: "I know this isn't fun to go through right now, but I refuse to let you stay in this state of despair because you are God's daughter and He accepts you and loves you and couldn't be prouder of you." Acknowledging their feelings as real, showing you understand...*but not allowing them to stay in self-pity, instead calling them back to His love by speaking truth over them.* This, to me, lines up much better with wanting God's will for that person. This is true love.

A real-life example of someone accessing this love lifestyle

I love God's Word for so many reasons. We get to see Jesus and other New Covenant believers just like ourselves (well, maybe I'm not a super highly educated tentmaker who starts a riot every time I enter a new city, but close enough) who all have their issues, but still consistently live from the place of loving the world around them as God loved them first. Church history is full of them too. But encountering a present-day follower of Jesus walking in this kind of grace often hits home in a way that makes even more of a lasting impact.

One great example is a pastor I'll call Sean that I met on a mission trip overseas.

We stayed at his house for one week of our mission. At first glance, nothing stood out about him. Soft-spoken, overdue for a haircut; nobody would call him impressive by the world's standards.

And yet, over the course of this week, what I saw in him can be called nothing less than mind-blowing. He lived like Jesus all the time. Driving our bus, already late for a ministry program, coming across three shady-looking strangers next to a broken-down car? Sean without hesitation stops to help them fix their engine...because *of course he does.* A group of forty hitchhikers want to join our already-full sixteen passenger bus? Hop aboard! Local hospital (in a poor, rural section of the country, mind you) only lets you get your arm jabbed with a needle to provide blood for needy patients once every 120 days? Obviously, Sean tries to sneak back in after 30! When he saw we were having trouble packing some of our clothes and toiletries for the trip home, there was no showmanship or maneuvering on his end. He looked me in the eyes and said with total sincerity, "If you wanted to leave some of that excess stuff, it would really be a blessing to the people." Sean and I served side by side for that week to accomplish the same mission. Yet there existed a clear difference between what he walked in and my reality at that time. I couldn't put my finger on it for years. It wasn't until I looked back at this trip post-grace conversion that it hit me. I realized I had chosen to do good works—build a Bible school, do a VBS program for local children, share the gospel in the villages—not because I had to do these things to earn salvation, but because that's what someone who loved Jesus should do. Faith without works is dead, right?

The problem that faced me is that it remained a mental assertion that I loved Jesus. It was still willpower that drove me to do these good works. It came from a rightly motivated spirit that occasionally experienced His heart in worship or prayer...but I knew I still lacked what Sean had.

I lived my life as a born-again, Spirit-filled Christian. I pastored a successful youth ministry. I walked and talked things that were true and even biblical. It was never "works" to earn God's love or forgiveness. Those were, of course, free gifts. But I saw in Scripture and the few like Sean who seemed to "get it" that if you were truly saved, works would accompany that. You weren't "proving you loved Jesus," but if you sincerely loved Jesus, your life would express it.

Now I see how my understanding of the Word and the way I lived out my legitimate salvation—and taught searching teens to do the same—can only be described as incomplete. As my friend Justin Kendrick says, "Identity comes before activity." Being secure in our identity as God's sons and daughters doesn't negate doing good works; the opposite is actually true. Almost all of us know a church that does many nice things to benefit society but still feels empty of the passionate love of God. Believe me, for every two or three churches like that there is another one where they sit around getting "drunk in the Spirit" all the time and go years without leading anyone to Jesus. Followers of Christ are called to actively engage people with His love that continually overflows our hearts. One interpretation of "righteousness" is "acts of kindness." *But the "doing" has to come from what He has already done in us.*

Maybe you've heard the quote, "Evangelism (Christians sharing God's love with people who don't yet know it) is just one beggar telling another beggar where to find bread." Many people I respect have taught this, and I agree we need the perspective that we're not superior or condescending when discussing our faith with others. My heart to reach lost sons comes from the fact that God loved me back when I lived as one myself!

However, in the bigger picture, I'm not a beggar anymore! I am completely dependent on Him for my daily bread, but I eat with Him at the table as His son. Here's how my buddy Jonathan and I see it:

> Evangelism is one beggar—who has been adopted as
> a son by the King, had his Father put royal robes of
> righteousness on him, and given unlimited feasts at
> His table—going back to the other beggars he used
> to look for bread with and excitedly telling them (in
> love, empty of pride) that the King wants to adopt
> them as sons and daughters too!

I never had a conversation with Sean about this, but his
life shouted the fact that he knew his identity as a son of
the King.

Taking Selfies

What is the opposite of love? Many would say "hate"
(thanks, Sesame Street book of opposites), but I make a
case for "selfishness." There's a preacher you may have
heard of named Dan Mohler. He talks about how *all* sin is
self-seeking, self-centered, self-preservation, stand up for
yourself, "me myself and I!"

Think about it—when Adam and Eve willfully dis-
obeyed a God who only loved them, what did they do
when He came to seek them out and spend time in relationship? They ran and hid: self-defense, self-preservation.
It's so easy to say, "Oh, Adam and Eve, how silly they acted,"
when we do the exact same thing. How do people respond
almost without fail when someone tells them they did a
bad thing? Immediately start making excuses, standing
up for their decision, trying to protect themselves. "*Well,
Jenny, I guess this church isn't very loving anymore. Let's
try the one on the other side of town!*" Come on, we've all
been there!

God says deny your*self*, pick up your cross, and follow
Me! What are we denying? Only the things that we weren't

created for anyway! We only lay down the rights, the habits, and the mind-sets that we inherited in man's fall. We have all been trained in them since birth: Stand up for yourself! If someone does you wrong, get them back or cut them off! We have been taught that anger and frustration are normal, that they are part of standing up for your rights! Jesus can say "deny yourself" *because you were never made for this in the first place!* Salvation occurs not when a person repeats a prayer, but when the nature of God is restored in them. We are not saved merely to house Him, but to become one with Him. And who is "Him"? The Bible says God is love. We are one with Him; therefore, we are to become love to those around us!²

We have become so self-righteous that we think our call to "speak the truth in love" means to blast someone over an issue we don't currently struggle with in our own life. Tacking on "you know I love you" at the end of a demeaning rant doesn't make it loving!

Does anyone know any Christians that feel called to a ministry of "arguments on the Internet"? Has there been one true salvation as the result of this? Even one changed mind on a single issue? *"Well, I have to stand up for the truth, you know. This stranger on Facebook has a clear misunderstanding of what God is all about. She thinks He's angry, intolerant, and condescending to women. This rant about all the commandments she's broken will open her blind eyes for sure!"*

Be honest; has anyone ever argued someone away from their point of view and closer to Jesus? *"But if we don't speak up we are hiding our light and compromising truth, and America will fall!"* No, quite the opposite. I see a place where people who have had "I am holy" spoken over them by their Father, unafraid of being accused of "compromising truth," who boldly and lovingly reach out as Jesus did. As we let our light shine, America (and any other nation) can be awakened once again to the gospel of love, grace...and Truth.

I hold that when the Bible says "the truth will set you free," the "truth" that the Lord mentions does not necessarily equal "accurate statements." Here's a test to demonstrate for anyone who has ever encountered middle school age youth in any capacity: when an adolescent girl tells an adolescent boy he is annoying. Might that be an accurate statement? Nearly always. But is it the truth that sets him free? Hardly. Has there ever been a twelve-year-old boy that responded to "You're so annoying!" with "Wow, thank you for your honesty. I never realized my behavior could be interpreted as obnoxious to those around me. You care about me enough to point this out; therefore I repent, and will never act that way again." Isn't it an almost 100 percent certainty that he will respond with a laugh, and then *repeat or even escalate the exact same annoying behavior?* The truth that sets people free speaks to people's created value (covered in detail in Chapter 6). Saying something "true," on the other hand, often simply reinforces the toxic issue they are currently dealing with, as our thirteen-year-old friend demonstrates to us.

I think we all would honestly admit that telling someone they will go to hell is equally ineffective, for the same reasons. *Oh, you're one of those liberal universalists who cares more about being politic...* OK, I'm going to cut you off there. You're wrong. Hell is real, and the ultimate destination for anyone who rejects God's offer of salvation. Now you tell me, how many people have come to know Jesus by someone leading with that information? I've never seen or heard of even one. Maybe you have heard of a few, but can we at least establish it hasn't led to any significant impact in America thus far in the last fifty years?

In the documentary *Father of Lights*, a "you're going to hell if you don't repent of your sins" type street preacher admits that, in over ten years of using these methods, he has never seen anyone saved. He did hear about one salvation that may have happened a few years back from one of his comrades.[3]

But even if nobody ever responds the way we want, it's our mission to speak truth! It's all about our heavenly reward, not how people look at us in this life. Let's not get this twisted. There are many who will reject the true gospel, and yes, great is our reward for sharing it anyway. But if our churches are going for one, two, three years without seeing even one new believer emerge, it is long past the time for us to take a look at our methods. There are an increasing number of churches that throw out truth in the name of "being loving," and it's just as wrong…but for many of us, the main problem is throwing out love in the name of "standing on the truth."

Actually, we want to be like Jesus. He wasn't afraid to "tell it like it is!" My friend, every time in Scripture that I see Jesus tell a person to "stop sinning," He first wins their heart with an incredible act of love. Recall the time He stopped a vicious attack on the woman caught in adultery, saving her life and driving off her attackers with supernatural wisdom. Then, He powerfully declared that He did not condemn her, speaking to how much He valued her as a person. Then He told her to go and sin no more. How would we dare to presume the right to speak truth like our Savior without first allowing His amazing love to be displayed through us?

Now, Something We Can All Agree On: Politics!

Hey, I know I haven't been overly constructive so far, but all of that aside, this is a pretty radical book. Just promise you're not going to mess it up by bringing politics into it!

Touché. How about if I use politics as a lightning rod to draw attention to a more important point about love? It's a big issue in the American church today. On one end of the spectrum there are faith groups that campaign on every issue, endorse their favorite candidate, and really make it clear which side they believe God is on. At the other extreme, certain churches teach that politics itself is flawed beyond redemption, and because it's "of this world" it's wrong to even vote.

As with most issues, I try to find the biblical balance and practice accordingly. I have come to believe that a level of political involvement is certainly important. We all know certain harmful decisions in history that seemingly happened because the church was "asleep," and other positive developments that occurred through the activism of God's people, both spiritual and practical. One of my friends is very gifted in this area and is visibly impacting society in ways that line up with the kingdom.

However, I do question whether much of our time spent in "political involvement" would be better served by pouring out God's love on the people around us every day in fresh, creative ways.

I live in Connecticut, arguably the most socially liberal of the blue states. Yet when they were considering giving legal recognition to homosexual unions a few years back, the politically active Christians responded in throngs. There were months of newsletters, e-mail blasts—I even think I saw a commercial in prime time. This all led up to a dual rally in front of the Capitol at which there were over two thousand concerned *Connecticut* citizens in favor of traditional marriage. I don't have exact numbers, but there were clearly less than a hundred protesting in favor of attempting to change the very definition of marriage by changing the laws.

Our noble representatives looked upon these demonstrations, reflected on the sincere hearts of over two thousand constituents that sought to maintain their Bible's definition of marriage, and overwhelmingly voted to change the laws.

Were all those hours campaigning a total waste? Or would it have been "giving up" for those who were so passionate to "defend truth" to just let the legislature take its course?

I have come to the conclusion that love is a much better weapon to wage war against that darkness than political signs.

Hey, I was one of those demonstrators, and I felt like I did so with a loving spirit! Can't you do both? I'm actually in favor of operating in love...but I just feel like laying down my picket sign would be abandoning truth.

Sure, you can do both. Everything is permissible, not everything is beneficial. I'm looking at results here. What would impact our nation in a way that would promote God's true kingdom the most? We need to get to the point where "you can love without diluting truth" doesn't even need to be said. It needs to become absolutely normal.

Wallace Henley awakens us to the need to be "militant" with only one agenda: love. "If the Church wants to get in the face of homosexuals, it must first wash the feet of homosexuals. The Church *should* be in the face of the monstrous practice of abortion on demand. She wins the right to do this when she cares for unwed mothers and their babies; when she helps heal those who have had abortion, and bear the spiritual and emotional scars."[4]

"That's a great theory, Mike, but it doesn't happen like that in the real world." Alan Hirsch would disagree. His revolutionary book *The Forgotten Ways* addresses a church that did just this:

> The first church plant was in [Melbourne's] red-light district, and was called Matthew's Party. This was a "street church" focused on reaching drug addicts and prostitutes. But with the subsequent sending out of our street-culture people, the sending church... underwent a transformation... [the church] was fairly unique, possibly even in world context, in that up to 40 percent of the community came from the gay and lesbian subcultures. What made this the more unique was that we did not take a politically correct, pro-gay stance, theologically speaking, but graciously called all people into a lifelong following of Jesus.[5]

That's what I'm talking about! A radical display of the love of God hand in hand with standing on truth! Hirsch goes on to describe how for some, this took the form of lifelong celibacy, while others pursued heterosexual relationships.[6]

My main premise in this book remains this: someone that deep into that kind of lifestyle can only get the will and desire to live celibate or pursue heterosexual relationships from one catalyst. That's having their world turned upside down by the unconditional love of Jesus.

"OK, so you read a book about something that happened on a distant continent. This is America, get real!"

You are aware that cynicism is not a gift of the Spirit, right? But since you mention it, I have seen this up close and personal as well.

A little while back, I took a year off from ministry and felt led to live in an apartment on the beach in California during that time. (Sometimes we make it seem really, really hard to follow the call of God on our lives. This was *not* one of those times.)

During that year, my church garnered several attacks for being "hateful and intolerant" simply for publicly sharing what the Word says about marriage. There was a protest that began in front of the church with a ginormous flag, insulting signs, and some people yelling angry slogans into megaphones. Several pastors and other staff members had a choice: get offended and "stand up for our rights" by responding in kind, or recognize we laid down the right to be offended when we started following Jesus, and pour out His compassion on them instead. They chose the #iamholy option, and slipped into the crowd to love on people. They passed out bottles of ice cold water, struck up friendly conversations, and even helped them carry their flag (folded up, of course) to the main rally in the center of town. As they turned to head back, they were asked, "Who are you guys, anyway?" "Oh," said one of the pastors, "we work at that church you were protesting."

Pretty intolerant, right? Come on! Don't you think that small but powerful act of love was a little more effective than bringing out our own megaphones and having a counter-protest? The email sent the next day by one of the rally leaders drives this home. It stated that although they believed they would never agree on the issue . . . they would also *never again accuse that church of being hateful!*

*Hugely important note: If anyone reading this currently

lives in any sort of lifestyle that isn't celibate or one-man, one-woman marriage, please keep reading. I don't assume you're necessarily looking for "healing"; and I wouldn't ask you through the medium of a book to even consider making any changes without first knowing the consuming love of God I keep talking about.

Delivering the word of God is one of the few things in life I take extremely seriously. I believe He prompted me to write these things the way I have—focusing briefly on those one or two issues to the exclusion of many others— for the sole purpose of opening your heart to His love. I apologize for the evils done in the name of "defending truth." A large focus of my life mission is to do my part to redeem the body of Christ to be known by what we *are* for—His radical love that sets us free from those things we hate about ourselves—and not what we think we're supposed to be against.*

I don't have to get into detail about what my conversations on hot-button issues looked like before grace. Suffice to say, I made sure not to "hide out" or "withhold the truth." And they never led anyone to change their lifestyle or want to know more of what the Word says. I can tell you what they look like now:

> Person living a certain lifestyle (already defensive): Oh, you're a Christian? Well, why don't you share what your opinion is on this marriage issue?

> Me: Well, I believe what the Bible says…

> Person (offended, ready to prove their point): So you think I'm abnormal! You think I'm going to hell! All you bigots are the same. How can you possibly still believe that stuff in the twenty-first century?

> Me: Actually, I was going to say: I believe what
> the Bible says…that Jesus loves you so much. He
> created you as a son of the living God. I believe He
> wants to show you His love today.

(This next part only works if you believe the Holy
Spirit speaks supernaturally through God's people today—
like He did through Jesus, Elijah, Peter, and others in
the Bible—if you allow Him to do so, and of course, if
He wills it at this moment. We have found in so many
cases, He does. At "worst" you can stop right there after
delivering the most loving declaration they've ever heard
from a Christian.)

> Me (continued): In fact, He was there that night you
> were a kid when you found out your dad was leaving
> your family. When your world fell apart and you
> asked out loud if anyone cared…do you remember
> that unexplainable feeling of peace and acceptance?
>
> Person (choked up): How…how did you know that?
>
> Me: I didn't. That was God, and He's reminding you
> right now that He's always loved you fiercely and
> wants to heal those hurts you've kept hidden inside.

Now that's a campaign we can throw our support behind.
When we listen to God speak over us—"I love you, son. I
adore you, daughter"—we begin to recognize that through
what He did, #iamholy, and let the Holy Spirit begin to
convict us in regard to righteousness. And although
Jesus certainly has the ability to appear supernaturally to
people, it's safe to say 99.9 percent of the time lost sons
and daughters only get introduced to His love through us,
the "found" sons and daughters! We can hate sin all we

want but if we're not loving the person first, foremost, and relentlessly, then nobody will ever see in us a reason to leave their current lifestyle to pursue Him.

The kindness of God leads us to repentance. When I lay down my right to demand that people meet my expectations before showing them His unconditional love, something supernatural happens. The true conviction of the Holy Spirit begins to bring change. And if we have proven that we are *for* that person regardless of what issues they currently struggle with, often they grant us the amazing privilege of speaking into their life.

And often, the first step toward showing His love to people—as overly simplistic or clichéd as it may sound—is a sincere smile. I am holy, I am loved, I am loving…and I am happy.

Chapter 4
I AM HAPPY

We [Christians] owe the world
an encounter with Jesus.
—BILL JOHNSON

[Since we owe the world an
encounter with Jesus], we don't have
the right to have a bad day!
—TODD WHITE

EVERY DAY IS A GOOD DAY. SERIOUSLY?

IF YOU HAD told me two years ago that you never had a bad day, I would have assigned you one of two labels: fake or delusional.

To my mind, you were likely fake—lots of gritting your teeth, suppressing stress and frustration deep inside, forcing phony smiles, and describing yourself as "blessed and highly favored!"

The other option is that you lived in a fantasy world of denial. "Every day is a good day...because I have forty billion dollars in the bank to buy Evander Holyfield's mansion and install my own personal In-N-Out Burger!"

(Just so you know, that's pretty close to an actual phone request I got when I worked to help manage people's retirement money a few years back. It was my first day taking calls; because of God's grace it was not the last).

(While I'm on the subject, I think Evander should pen an autobiography called #iamholyfield. Who's with me?)

Basically, I thought being happy all the time meant ignoring reality in one of those two forms—being fake, or being in denial. Honestly, as Christians that should not be the case. We must acknowledge the reality we see all around us.

The life-transforming realization is that through Christ in us, *we live in a higher reality.*

I love the example in Romans 4:17–21. Abraham had been given a promise from God: that He had made him the father of many nations. Abe recognized that God "gives life to the dead and calls things that are not as though they are." The Bible says he faced the fact (this world's reality) that his body was as good as dead. He was neither fake nor delusional regarding the situation. Come on, he was 100 years old! He didn't try to "speak it into existence." He didn't walk around saying, "I'm thirty, I'm thirty." Abraham acknowledged the current facts accurately *at the same time he was fully persuaded that God's higher reality superseded what everyone saw in the physical realm!* He put his faith in truth louder than circumstances, refusing to waver through unbelief.

BLAME IT ON THE RAIN

Listen, friends, even mainstream psychology teaches that it's not what happens to us, it's our response that determines success. Jesus, in Matthew 5, comments that it rains on the righteous and the unrighteous all the same.

There's a dangerous false gospel that basically says once we receive salvation, it never rains again. All we have to look forward to are financial windfalls, favor (in the sense of, say, being supernaturally first in every line you ever would have had to wait in), and immunity from any of life's difficulties. Other than the really "big dogs" who profit indefinitely from this message, I have not seen a disciple of this kind of teaching last more than a couple of years. By the twenty-sixth time they don't claim what they've named (i.e., a private jet), it's off to disillusionment with Christianity and/or joining a new spiritualish belief system that carries promises to "fill their vats to overflowing."

However, there's another false gospel that may be even more dangerous because it's endorsed by more credible people and movements: if you truly follow Christ as Lord and Savior, get ready for the rain, baby! This one interprets the "narrow road" talked about in the Bible as one chock full of suffering, pain, and self-denial in the sense of denying yourself any fun, pleasure, or happiness. It teaches that things are bad and only getting worse now, but if we just hold on until Jesus gets back, it will all be worth it.

Derek Levendusky states, "If you want to know what the Bible says, find out what the Bible also says."[1] I like that a lot, simply because we all gravitate toward picking the verses that seem to clearly support our current beliefs, and dismiss or attempt to explain away the ones that seem to stand in our way. (*"Oh, that. Uh...scholars recently discovered we've been interpreting it wrong for the last two thousand years. Who's with me?"*)

The whole of Scripture on this particular subject seems to be summed up in what Jesus said to His followers: "In this world, you will have trouble. But take heart! *I have overcome the world*" (John 16:33). Here's the Pope Massé commentary: There are going to be times of rain no matter what. But Jesus is so much bigger than even the biggest storm. Sometimes He will supernaturally command them to be still (remember Peter), and other times there's a shipwreck coming but you will not be harmed (our good buddy Paul). All of that pales in comparison to His love for us. If we make Him our focus, we can immensely enjoy the sunny days...and while we acknowledge the reality of the rainstorms, they do not cause us to lose our joy or get off course in His plan for our lives. In fact, we will come out of them with stronger faith, character, and spiritual sensitivity because we chose to pass these tests by following faith over feelings. How else does it make sense to "count it all joy, brothers and sisters, when you endure tests and trials of many kinds"?

IF YOU'RE HAPPY AND YOU KNOW IT, TELL YOUR FACE

This brings us to one of my heroes, King David. Scripture is divinely inspired, and there's a reason why every single word has been included in the Bible. In fact, I'll talk later about how some of David's most desperate prayers impacted me powerfully through a time of intense testing in my life. (I am all about honesty and transparency in prayer, which Dave pretty much mastered.) However, I want to address something I have heard taught in more than one church that neglects a seriously important context regarding some of his statements in Psalms. More specifically, sermons referring to his comments about how it stinks that God feels so far away, how it stinks that so many people hate him, how his life generally stinks. I've even heard David described (again, by more than one preacher) as bipolar due to how quickly the tone of his prayers shifts from joyous to defeated—and sometimes back again.

Many of us have taken this and said something like: "Wow, I can totally relate to how David was feeling there! Thank You, Lord, for letting me know that it's completely normal to question You and complain about how people treated me today! I must be a man after Your own heart!" There's one major issue with this mind-set: *David did not have Jesus Christ living inside him.* He *was* a man after God's own heart and is a great example to us in many ways. But David lived smack dab in the middle of the old Covenant. If we decide to live as slaves to our emotions and the situations that face us in life, that will put us right back there, when we have by God's grace the opportunity to enter the new, better Covenant—the one God made with Jesus and we can enter into through faith. The covenant leading to the lifestyle where Jesus Himself can manifest through our very thoughts, words, and actions—the same Jesus from Chapter 1 of Mark! Let's take a look.

HOW TO RESPOND TO TOUGH CIRCUMSTANCES, JESUS-STYLE

Jesus has just been baptized by the Holy Spirit, passed His tests in the desert, and been released to start ministering in power. Then, He gets a piece of terrible news. John had been put in prison. This is huge! His cousin and likely childhood friend—the "greatest man born of woman," who had overseen His very baptism—had just received, in essence, a death sentence.

Let's pick up in Mark 1:14. Multiple choice:

A. When Jesus heard John had been put in prison...He wrote a Psalm lamenting

> how scary His enemies had become, how
> depressed that made Him, and where, oh
> where was God?

This seems like it might have been David's response on some days. Thank God we have a better way!

> B. When Jesus heard John had been put in
> prison...He went on Facebook and posted,
> "I hate my life." Then for good measure, He
> tweeted, "Some people are totally rude.
> you'll get yours #jerks," then high-fived Peter
> and said "they know who they are."

Is this not how many in our current youth ministries—and dare I say, churches—would respond?

> C. After John had been put in prison...He went
> into Galilee, proclaiming the good news of
> God! "The kingdom of God is near."

That was His response! It's unfathomable in our own strength. The "wisdom" of the world might even call Jesus "uncaring." *Your cousin just got sentenced to death, man. You're going to go preach a sermon?* We know from the story of Lazarus and other accounts that He experienced grief and anguish. It's pretty safe to surmise He didn't take this as a pleasant development. But even the worst of circumstances couldn't take the joy of the Lord from His heart. Nothing could send Him into self-pity or distract Him from declaring the good news.

Well, duh, of course He could stay focused on God regardless of the circumstances. He was God! I can never aspire to that.

Yes and no. Yes in the sense that we are not, and will never be, God or His equals in Lordship. I emphatically disagree, however, that we can't aspire to that sort of focus on the Father no matter what goes on around us. Here's the deal: Jesus never stopped being 100 percent God. At the same time, He was 100 percent human. The Word makes it clear He was tempted in every way…just like we are! We like to equate that to our struggles with classic sins such as lust and lying; but wouldn't it also encompass discouragement, hopelessness, and being a slave to emotions and circumstances as well? I'm not trying to start a theological debate here—I've made it clear I no longer have time for that sort of thing. But we can say that He chose to lay down many benefits of His God-ness *in the sense* that He chose to live a human life totally dependent on His heavenly Father. Philippians 2:6–8 and John 5:19 speak about how He humbled Himself, made Himself a servant, and could only do what He saw God the Father doing. This is how we can legitimately follow Him as our ultimate example.

How was that kind of surrender and dependency on God possible? Most would say a combination of constant communion with the Spirit and withdrawing to lonely places to pray and "see what His Father was doing." And I agree. But I also believe those things are impossible over the long term for us without what happened to Jesus first.

Before any recorded signs and wonders, before any mention of making disciples, there was His baptism. The incident where God the Father spoke and said: "This is my beloved Son, in whom I am well pleased." What was the Father pleased with? All the converts Jesus had made? The miracles He had performed? We have no record in the Bible or any other legitimate source that any of those things had occurred up to that point.

The Father was pleased with *Him*. He was His Son. Unlike us, Jesus was the firstborn—the only one that didn't have to be adopted in. But that was the proclamation fathers made in that culture at the end of the adoption ceremony. Everything our Savior did from that point on was loving, because God the Father had confirmed to Christ (as well as everyone privileged to witness the moment) that His Son was loved.

When God speaks over you and calls you His beloved son or daughter, in whom He is well pleased...that's it, my friend. Nothing can steal that joy. Temporary unpleasant circumstances no longer dictate my happiness level. He alone does. I'm not talking about a head knowledge or mental assent that God loves me, or that I'm His child, or any church-ism along those lines. I lived and ministered there for years with little to show for it in terms of long-term fruit.

I'm referring to the heart-shaking encounter with His Father's heart.

My Earliest Memory of the Father's Heart

I lived in a small home in a working class neighborhood until I was twelve. Behind our house was a patch of woods that spanned roughly fifty yards, and behind that resided one of the most dangerous housing complexes in the city. (A visibly shaken babysitter once told me the gunshot sound I'd just asked about was a dumpster lid slamming down.)

As soon as my brother and I were old enough to play in the yard, my dad put up a tall, thick wooden fence for protection. He made it very clear if we hit or kicked a ball over that fence, well—I hope you feel a sense of closure, because it's gone.

And, sure enough, several Wiffle balls, Nerf balls, and even a Frisbee met their early demises over the next few months. It was the price of energetic fun, and we were fine with it.

Then one day, my special red ball went over the fence. You know how that goes—for whatever inexplicable reason, a kid decides *this* toy is the most amazing toy ever invented, more so than the other equivalent or even more expensive ones. That described the red ball that six-year-old me played with every day. Until the day my kickball skills finally superseded my common sense. I can see it in slow motion to this day: Ol' Red flying through the air. ("It's gonna hit the fence, it's gonna hit the fence, no, no, *NO!!!! IT WENT OVER!!!!*)

I was devastated. In just two years time, my older (and less compliant, I suppose) self would have jumped over the fence, retrieved the ball, and jumped right back into our yard. But at age six, this was the end of the world.

I moped around for a few days, barely finding solace in the orange ball—which was in every other way identical to the red one—that we still possessed. Or my Huffy bicycle, Pogo Ball, handheld football game with blinking red dots (getting enough nostalgia points with the "we grew up in the eighties" crowd yet?), or anything for that matter.

Then a few days later when I had finally forgotten about the ball and moved on, I came home to see my father standing in the living room with a big smile on his face. He pulled his arm from behind his back—*and there was my red ball!* I don't mean he bought a replacement; this was *my* ball. In a millisecond, I knew what this meant—he had jumped over the forbidden fence himself because he knew how much this particular toy meant to me.

I'm trying to convey the overwhelming sense I had of being loved by my dad at that moment. I ran and threw my arms around him. I felt like he was my buddy, my protector, and someone who would do anything for me.

Early in the process of my grace conversion, I had a dream that basically replayed this event from twenty-plus years earlier. I felt like God was showing me all the times He "retrieved a ball" for me and my heart was overtaken by His love. Though emotions fade and feelings change, every time I reminded myself of my heavenly Father's heart toward me, joy increased.

That's the place where the joy of the Lord is my strength. Never having a bad day doesn't depend on pleasant circumstances or even whether I feel joyful. It's the immovable knowledge that He remains joyful, and His heart is for me. That's where I draw my strength from. Period.

I have been to countless Christian gatherings where we either 1) verbally vomit on each other—complaining and trying to top each other's "bad day" testimony—under the guise of "being real," or 2) pasting on a fake smile and pretending everything is OK so not to "bring anyone down" before we enter into worship, where we thank God for blessing us while thinking how un-blessed we feel! Let's address the misguided thinking behind "being real."

"I'M JUST BEING REAL"

Remember, true happiness through the #iamholy mindset is about acknowledging the world's reality but living according to our God's higher one. Being real (in this sense) doesn't earn you any points with me anymore, and it certainly doesn't inspire any lost sons and daughters to want what you have. I hesitate to speak for God, but if you're "being real" with Him about how negative your situation seems without following up by asking Him to help replace that perspective with the truth that He is so much greater than these things, and He lives inside you with the grace and power to walk according to how powerless they actually are—it's tough to see how that pleases Him either.

Hey now, no condemnation here—He is still completely pleased with *you*. That's kind of the point of this book. He accepts who you are through Christ in you, and no amount of whining on our end will change that. It's just as Graham Cooke says, "Aren't we supposed to be dead to this stuff? Well then, let's flippin' die already!" (If you can hear *that* with no condemnation, friend, we are getting somewhere.)

For years, I thought talking about my bad day or letting people know I struggled with a certain issue was "being real." People who didn't know Jesus would appreciate that I didn't pretend everything was OK like a big fake, and it might open up an opportunity to dialogue about God. Then what? Maybe I can casually work hell into the conversation and they'll think it's cool that I'm not going there—but they are? My life looks just like theirs but they love how I cling to the bumper sticker promise that "I'm not perfect...just forgiven"? I guess I didn't think that through.

Everyone I knew thought I was great at "keeping it real," but it really left nothing in my life that pointed to a more excellent way. I swore and gossiped less than my non-Christian friends, but those "blatant" sins aside, we really responded the same way to life's trials.

Then I learned the difference between fake and practice. Fake is pasting on a fake smile and trying to convince yourself through gritted teeth that everything is great. Practice, though, involves recognizing that everything around you may not be peachy keen, but it doesn't change the truth that the joy of the Lord is my strength! Ergo, even though I don't *feel* like it, I'm going to smile! And when we take a step of faith, the feelings almost always follow that. Even the Association for Psychological Science is catching on. A 2012 Study shows that "smiling under pressure can play a part in reducing the intensity of a body's stress response."[2] #iamholy: good for your heart!

MAGNIFYING GLASS

Whether it rains or the sun shines, whether circumstances are pleasant or unpleasant, what our lives will manifest depends on our response! Do we adopt the mind-set, "I'll never beat this sin"? Do we focus on the four "bad" things that have happened to us today even before we got to drink our morning coffee? What are we magnifying? Cooke explains that we were created to magnify. That means you either see some thing bigger than it actually is, or you see some One as big as He actually is!

Who taught us to respond to unpleasant situations with unrighteous anger, depression, brooding, unforgiveness, choosing isolation from Christian brothers and sisters, and even forcing ourselves to apathetically sit through another church service where "we don't feel it"? Can we agree it wasn't Holy Spirit? Everything I've ever seen in the Word, victorious examples in church history, and personal experience shows me He does not teach any of these things. Responses of love, joy, patience, kindness, self-control—now, these sound more up His alley.

So...those negative reactions must have been taught to

us by the world. Our whole lives, we've been trained to react to a situation like this: sin against us produces sin in us! [3]

My friends, if you interact with people on any sort of regular basis, you will be served a heaping bowl of "wrong" on many occasions. It doesn't change Jesus! I'm so pumped to see a generation stand up and say "I am sick of sin against me producing sin in me" and choose to surrender to the grace of Christ in us, the hope of glory instead.

You don't understand, Pastor Mike. What she did totes deserved what I said about her on Twitter! Well...first of all, I likely do understand. Nearly every situation you can explain to me where someone did you wrong either happened to me personally, or to someone I had a close relationship with as we walked through it together. But let's just say you're right this time and I don't understand. Guess who does? The One who lives inside you and gives you the grace to allow Him to live through you. The One who said "turn the other cheek."

Wait, didn't He say "turn the other cheek...unless they did something horrible and really deserve to be smacked down"? No. *Are you sure it wasn't, "Christians should be servants, but not doormats"?* Positive. It was "turn the other cheek"—with no ifs, ands, or buts about it.

If we start to walk in love—if we can encourage ourselves that #iamholy because God meets all my needs according to His glorious riches in Christ Jesus—then it becomes impossible for anyone to wound us emotionally! Does this sound good, woman of God? That verse that says I am accepted by God makes it completely nonsensical for me to think someone rejected me!

Oh, but that co-worker of mine makes me so angry!

Really? He "makes you angry"? He kidnaps your family and calls with instructions: "Manifest anger right now, or kiss little Johnny good-bye"? No, you choose to be angry. That's slavery to both the other person and your emotions. If I let you hurt, offend, or anger me, I am your slave. How can I then love you? It's only if I laid down those rights, if I lost my "life" to find it in Christ, that it's possible to manifest His love and forgiveness instead of toxic emotions.

If you have put your faith in Jesus, you are dead to sin. You cannot live in it any longer. Everything the world has taught you is now submitted to the Lordship of "Christ in me, the hope of glory."

How dare you, iamholy boy! I believe Jesus lives inside me too, but you don't know the extent of the pain they caused me. All we are actually saying is, "I want to hold on to this pain because the wisdom of the world has trained me to believe the lie that they 'deserve' it. I know the Holy Spirit in me can lead me to become love, but that would be too good for this person I see as an enemy."

Yeah, well you don't know how it feels! Show me once in the Bible where it says we should be led by our feelings! We're led by the Holy Spirit, God's Word, and faith, not feelings. When we start to believe truth instead of what the world trained us to feel, all of a sudden the real enemy doesn't have access anymore.

But my mom taught me my feelings are always valid! And he hurt my feelings!

There's only one reason for that, and I'll let a man of God I highly admire address it:

> People have hurt feelings because they're immature, overly sensitive (usually due to past wounds that have not been healed but allowed to fester), self-centered, and carnal.
>
> —LEON VAN ROOYEN[4]

I implore you, friends, don't let that offend you! Let it be a wake-up call to run to the Father's heart and let His love and grace begin to accelerate the process of maturity as we receive from Him all needed healing. Every day we pray—and practice—living happy.

Dan Mohler says (and I paraphrase), "If you feel lost, you can go on a long 'journey,' with a need to constantly ask others for prayer so you can make it through. *Or* you can thank God you're not actually lost—destroy that lie with truth—and soon enough, the feeling goes away. It only hurts because we're thinking about our *self* and not the gospel. I have stopped crying (being hurt, angry, offended) *because* of other people, and now I just cry *for* them (get before God and pray that He reveals His passionate love to them) because they're the one who doesn't know who they are!"

THE MILLION DOLLAR QUESTION

"*Mike*," you're saying out loud this very moment (to the amusement of the other passengers on the plane), "*are you telling me you don't have any bad days?*" I tell you, friend, even if I haven't completely arrived yet, you better believe I am closer than I was six months ago. I'm closer than I was when I started writing this book—I can honestly say I'm closer than I was when I started writing this paragraph!

I don't mean there are no bad circumstances. As we know, they tend to come in bunches.

I also don't consider the unshakeable joy and peace as separate realities from occasions that carry legitimate grief or anguish. The "movie" of Jesus praying in the garden of Gethsemane doesn't include "Shiny Happy People" playing in the background. Yet it's clear He wasn't thrown off His mission—or into questioning God's love—by the temporary pain. (And the next day's "Why have You forsaken me" doesn't apply to us, by the way. Whether or not you believe the teaching that the Father turned away from Him in that moment—there's a strong case that Jesus was actually declaring the fulfillment of Psalms 22—scripture makes it clear that He will *never* leave or forsake us.)

Nowhere in the Bible do we see a promise of a life without pain. The promise is "no harm will befall you." I find a great description of the promise to be a place where the temporary pain of life doesn't harm, damage, or scar us. When a relative passes away, I grieve and miss being in relationship with them in this life, but it's from a place where His "peace that passes understanding" doesn't leave me for a moment. Real grief is not mutually exclusive from everlasting joy.

Additionally, the unending joy I have found in Christ actually partners with a real anguish for lost sons and daughters who have never known this happiness. #iamholy in regards to this issue says: I will never again cry (note—for those like me who never really were the cry-y type, this means "get bitter, hurt, or angry") *because* of someone else. I will only cry *for* them (again, not necessarily "cry" but "pray, cry out to God, or intercede").

When a friend abandons me, instead of falling apart, I let God heal my hurt quickly. I don't "need more time." I have Jesus! I then begin asking Him to bless and heal that friend in whatever place their hurt is coming from.

I consider a "bad day" one where we allow circumstances or people to drive us into discouragement, depression, unforgiveness, and similar toxic mind-sets. I can only remember a few days over the past year that could be described as "bad." That does not include the day of the phone call where I was told my brother had (temporarily) died. It certainly doesn't include the day six weeks after I had made it through mass layoffs at my job that they informed me I was let go too, with no severance package. Those were great days, because God met me there in ways He could not when everything was pleasant.

The bad days only include the few times I made the foolish decision to believe a lie and let circumstances speak louder than God's Word for a few hours. You know, that someone who wronged me deserved more than instant forgiveness. What they did was bad enough that I had the *right* to be hurt or frustrated.

Of course, Holy Spirit gently reminded me of the truth, and in every case within twenty-four hours I had repented and began running in grace again. And the last one of those occurrences becomes more of a distant memory every day!

Listen, as we pray and practice, this consistent flow of grace manifests stronger and stronger. But we all (especially those of us with young children) eventually get to a point where we hit the wall, so to speak. It's OK to take a step back, a deep breath, and ask Jesus for—as my son says after five jelly beans—"more please." (He says "mo peez." It's so cute. Or it was until he turned fifteen.) I (and those who are starting to run with this reality) don't pretend to have achieved a place in the Spirit by returning to faking or denial.

The joy of the Lord flows naturally as we pray and practice…until we hit a wall. Then, we get the great honor of running into His presence for more. Everything in this book comes from a place of 100 percent dependence on God, so it should be the easiest thing in the world to admit we're still totally dependent on Him for those extra doses of grace when needed.

So God continually pours into us the love, grace, and

joy to live sincerely happy. Where does it all come from? His love, poured into a heart that is devoted and passionate toward Him...

Chapter 5
I AM DEVOTED

It's the revelation of His love for us that
awakens our love for Him...His love incites
ours to the point where we don't have to
strive or struggle to live a life of passion.

—BANNING LIEBSCHER[1]

[You must have] continual public
confession of what you are and
what Jesus Christ is to you.

—JOHN G. LAKE[2]

M Y A.D.D. KICKED *in and I skipped ahead. Man,
this chapter is short!*
Ah, this was actually part of Chapter 6 that, as
the great theologian Bob (from Bob's Discount Furniture)
would say, "just kept growing and growing." Devotion is
so critical to the whole #iamholy lifestyle that I had to
commit a separate chapter to it!

I AM DEVOTED = I AM PASSIONATE

I think every Christian wants to be more devoted. The
problem has become that we think of "devoted" as a
description of someone resigned to keeping a vow they
may or may not feel like keeping anymore. Let's start
defining "devoted" as "passionately committed to someone
or something."

When we look at the whole of Scripture (not to mention

the only thing that actually works in real life), the complete statement #iamholy actually looks like this: "These holy things will naturally flow out of your life because you are completely consumed by love for Jesus that originates with the revelation of His firstlove, and are allowing Him to live and love God and others through you." (Hi, I'm run-on sentence!)

"But I don't *feel* consumed today," you might say. "Just push through that and do what you know is right," I likely would have replied before I discovered true grace. "It's like a marriage—we have some "wow" days and some "vow" days," I was always taught.

That is, some days we will feel love for God's Word and presence burning in our hearts—wow! You know, what I read jumps off the page and applies perfectly to what I am going through at the moment!

And some days we will have to bite the bullet and force ourselves to read the Bible and pray. I'm not feeling God's presence, or I'm not "getting anything out of" what I'm reading today—but I know it's the right thing to do, so I push through. We do these devotions even if we don't want to, or feel like it. We do it as a discipline because of the vow we made at salvation.

I now know that there is a place—without being fake, delusional, or in denial–where every day is a "wow" day.

Let me explain.

There is certainly a place for discipline in the Christian life. The problem is, we have taught in our messages and by example that "discipline" equals "chore." Listen, friends, if at any point deepening our relationship with Jesus amounts to a chore, the answer is not to "push through it"! The solution is to get before Him in a secret place of intimacy and cry out for Him to pour His grace and love into us. To begin to practice believing truth louder than circumstances!

A great real-life picture of this took place when my smokin' hot wife and I were in our engagement phase. For part of this season she lived three thousand miles away, so every time we talked on the phone we both entered "cloud nine" territory for the entirety of the call. We were overwhelmed by love, joy, and affection every time we made this connection. I remember often looking up and realizing two hours had passed by, lost in the encounter with my beloved.

Now imagine it is 7 p.m. I am completely comfortable on my Love Sac (the best piece of furniture ever devised—think part beanbag chair, part magic), with an ice cold Dr Pepper, watching the game. My phone rings in the other room. At that precise moment, does my body or mind "feel" like getting up and walking over there? Not really. But is it a "chore" when I know the pure joy of hearing the voice of the one I love, pouring out our hearts in a mutual desire to grow in intimacy is what awaits? As the great theologian Johnny from middle school youth group would say: "No way, man!"

There may be times when pulling out the Word and withdrawing to a lonely place to pray is not 100 percent what my body or mind feels like doing. In that sense, devotions involve discipline. But knowing that the One I love is calling to me, that a heart-to-heart connection that overwhelms me, sustains me, and revives me awaits means it is *never* a chore.

If you read the Bible like any book, or merely as a religious discipline, or because you're convinced it's the right thing to do, or because your mom or youth pastor thinks it's a good idea, you will certainly have days where you "don't get anything out of it." In fact, you'll likely have far more "vow" days than "wow" days. Most people who approach it this way end up feeling condemned and guilty at how they continually fall short, and shift to a halfhearted approach...or even abandon the pursuit altogether.

But if you go to God with a heart that is desperate to hear from Him—to get a deeper understanding of who He really is and who you really are—whether or not the words "jump off the page" or relate to "exactly what I'm going through," you are going to be encouraged.

Banning Liebscher also likens it to his earthly marriage:

> My marriage with my wife is not a marriage of disciplines. Although it would be untrue to say that every day of marriage is bursting with passionate love, I am married to my wife because I am fervently in love with her, not because I am in a business contract with her. It is true that love is a choice and not just a feeling, but I don't wake up every day saying "Today, I am going to choose to love my wife." My passion for my wife is what drives me as I walk out my desire to spend the rest of my life with her.[3]

Sustained devotion has to come out of a heart that has been touched by the passionate love and grace of God!

A New Perspective on Devotions

I have read John 1 over a hundred times in my life. Yet after my grace conversion, God spoke to me through it in a way that marked my morning devotional time forever. Jesus asks the disciples what they want from Him. Their response is simply, "Teacher, where are you staying today?"

How does He answer them? "Come, and you will see."

So they went and saw where He was staying, and they spent that day with Him.

The moment that revelation hit me, my devotional time changed forever. Now my heart strives every morning to lay my requests down. Everything I want to ask God about life, family, finances, ministry, etc. takes a backseat to "Jesus, where are You staying today?" To put it plainly, if that day's devotions involve me talking, here's what I say: "God, what are You saying? What do You want to do in me, and what do You want to do through me this day?" He then pours into me the grace I need for that time and place. The forgiveness I am going to need to grant someone at 2 p.m.—there's the grace for that at 7:30 a.m. I stay connected to Holy Spirit throughout the day as well, but this regular time in the "prayer closet" has become invaluable to consistently live out the truth that #iamholy.

DEVOTION LEADS TO HOLINESS

After fifteen years in youth ministry, you begin to notice a few trends. Virtually every time a young person opens up to say they've been struggling with a certain sin and/or apathy, guess what statement also accompanies that?

"*I'm just going to be real* (uh oh)...*I haven't been in the Word lately.*"

It's like every time someone tells me their foot hurts, I look down and say, "Um...of course it hurts. You've got a knife in it!"

The opposite also holds true. "*Pastor Mike, this week has been amazing. I've really been living victory to victory, not that everything happens the way I would like it to of course...but I've been able to keep my eyes on God and not lose my passion no matter what the situation!* (Wait for it…) *Also, my time with Jesus every morning has been awesome.*

Look, we all know "doing devotions" doesn't necessarily translate to "life of victory." That's not what I or these teens I'm describing are all about. Hopefully this chapter changes your perspective forever on what it means to follow Jesus's example and "withdraw to lonely places to pray." Intentional prayer and practice is the only way I've found in Scripture and experience to consistently live victorious.

Chapter 6
I AM VICTORIOUS
(ALTERNATE TITLE: I WIN)

You were not created to be dominated,
you were created to dominate over
the circumstances in your life.
—Daniel Park[1]

They overcame him by the Blood
of the Lamb and the word of their
testimony. They did not love their lives
so much as to shrink from death.
—Revelation 12:11

Courage is almost a contradiction in
terms; it means a strong desire to live
taking the form of readiness to die.
—Chesterton[2]

ONE CATALYST FOR this book was the hundreds of Christians I've met through the years—including myself for most of my life—who, when honest, express frustration that their lives do not seem to match the promises of the Bible. Experiential reality stood in stark contrast to the life of "victory to victory" that is ours, according to God's Word. We lived with a sincere love for God and desire to be more like Him but still tasted defeat every day to sin and the tests and trials of life. *That has begun to change.*

There's no "secret" to #iamholy. Yet one trait has started to stand out as common among everyone who does embrace a life of victory over circumstances: identity. The most important thing God speaks to us regards who He really is. The finished work of Christ in His death and resurrection is the foundation for everything written in this book. The second most important thing? *Who you really are.*

PERSPECTIVE IS EVERYTHING

I learned a lot about the importance of identity during that seminal moment in a young man's life: high school football. The three years before I got there were all losing seasons. They had talented players and coaches but couldn't break the expectation of another 3–7 or 4–6 season. That's just who they were.

But something happened that May that changed everything. The three guys that had been chosen as captains decided to adopt a new identity. When asked to rally the players at the end of spring practice, they explained the concept of FIDO. Forget It, Drive On. In essence, delete the past from our memories, and look forward with this understanding: *We are undefeated.*

Preseason practices carried a buzz that the veterans agreed had never before been present. Other students on-site to use the track or weight room would say stuff like, "Hey, you guys gonna do better than last year? That was pretty bad." The response: stare through them and simply reply, "We're undefeated."

Traditionally, the week before classes (and the football season) officially started, players snuck to "the hill" off to the side of the school grounds at night and spray-painted their super-cool nicknames next to their jersey numbers. This year, it simply read "10–0." Prophesy much?

We (that's right, I'm saying "we" even though I was a freshman that got no varsity action that year. It was definitely my tireless sideline support that produced the team's tipping point) refused to define ourselves by past performance and instead spoke, thought, and acted according to what we truly believed was our destiny. Every summer practice the captains reminded us we were to conduct ourselves on and off the field like the champions we had now morphed into. When the locker rooms opened up in September, you better believe "10–0" got plastered all over everything.

And guess what? As God is my witness, we went 10–0 that year. Each week looked different: some close games, some blowouts, even one where we had a crazy Hollywood-style comeback…but they all ended in a victory. It was inevitable! We already viewed ourselves as undefeated, so that's what manifested through us on the field.

Not only that, it completely changed the culture of the program. Over the course of my four years (the last two of which I actually contributed *on* the field at the varsity level), we actually obtained the best four-year record in the history of that high school. Thirty-five wins to only five losses, if memory holds.

Now, if a group of three brazen young men can start running their mouths and convincing a group of generally unmotivated teenagers that they are undefeated before they have seen any physical evidence to confirm it, how much more when the very Word of God Himself says, "No weapon forged against me will prevail"?

OK, even I have to admit that story gave me goose bumps. But if living victoriously and fearlessly is really an

identity thing, how are you going to tie that in to holiness?
You do recall the title of your book, right?

Let me respond by asking a question to all the long-time churchgoers reading this: Who has ever been taught "you're going to sin" (fail, fall, drop the ball, or any metaphor for choosing to think, speak, or act outside of God's will)? I remember one year at youth camp the whole theme of the final day's messages was, "You are going to fail. Just make sure to *fail forward.*" I understand the heart behind it, more or less: "You are going to leave camp on fire for God and committed to never sinning again. If you do choose to sin, though, don't get discouraged and throw out everything He did in you at camp; just be forgiven and get back on the path." As an experienced camp veteran, I agree with the noble motivation behind this, but I can also wholeheartedly confirm that it *doesn't work.*

When a preacher is pointing at us, reiterating over and over again, "You are going to fail," should any of us have been surprised when the net result was failure? Should we be shocked and appalled when well-known pastors "fall"? When every Christian we know defines themselves by their ability to "drop the ball"? Camp ends in early August, just in time for hundreds of young revivalists to be unleashed into their schools. Yet by December most if not all were back to living lives ranging from powerless to worldly to outright backslidden. It's the opposite of what happened with my football team. Their identity has been declared, confirmed, and practiced as "one who fails."

Come on, when every sermon about holiness has to throw in the disclaimer, "now, we're never going to be perfect in this life," and we drive around with bumper stickers that say "Christians aren't perfect...just forgiven," it can't be a surprise when the majority of us walk around defeated!

VICTORY IS MINE!

If you're not free from sin until you die, Jesus isn't your Savior. Death is.

—AUTHOR UNKNOWN

When the man of God says in Psalm 19:13, "Then will I be innocent, clear and blameless of transgression," I don't think he's claiming to achieve sinless perfection. But the context makes it clear: his heavenly Father has forgiven and set him free from his hidden faults and kept him from being ruled by willful sins.

Perhaps that's what devoted accountability looks like. When I ask one of my spiritual sons how his week is going, I'm not looking for a list of sins from the last few days. I honestly don't care about the time an impatient thought was entertained, or—Heavens to Betsy—a swear slipped out. Those things don't line up with his actual created value. I want to first celebrate how he's grown, what God has shown him, and other things that make this faith walk a great adventure. But when we do move to addressing "issues," my concern is for exposing hidden faults and helping him grasp the victory Jesus already won over willful sins.

Check out Romans 2—Paul turns the attention of his gospel-believing paisans to problems with stealing, adultery, and blasphemy, among other things. Then, in Romans 13, he addresses issues such as drunkenness, jealousy, and orgies. We'd have trouble referring to them as Christians, let alone not kicking them out of church.

And yet, look at Romans 15:14. "I am convinced you are full of goodness." Wait, what? On one hand: full of goodness. On the other hand: drunkenness and orgies. Does…not…compute.

Paul must have no recollection of what he dictated a few pages earlier. But the Holy Spirit inspires every word in the Bible, so that can't be the case. Could it be that Paul knew the truth, that when Jesus said "it is finished," He meant it? Maybe he learned, as I have, that when you're reminded of who you were created to be, those things you were created for are far more likely to manifest through you! If someone has made a declaration of faith in Jesus, there definitely exists a place to lovingly address character issues. But it *has* to be from that place of reminding them who they really are.

Paul brings the sins out of the darkness and exposes them to Light by explaining they are part of the old way of thinking and living. But he doesn't stop there. He tells the Roman Christians what God thinks of them, through what he thinks of them. They *are* full of goodness!

A New Take on Preaching Repentance

There's a story I've heard in several forms (unsure where it originated to give proper credit) that demonstrates this point really well. I'll present my funny yet powerful youth pastor version. Let's say a rich, prestigious princess of a random European country gets hit on the head with a chandelier while dancing at a ball. Diagnosis: instant amnesia. Somehow in the chaos of being ushered out to get medical attention, she accidentally gets on a plane instead. Because it's the only logical outcome, she lands in Hartford, Connecticut. Now she is hungry, dirty, and has no concept of her true identity. So she finds some people bound in poverty in a back alley eating trash from a dumpster. They make an uneasy alliance, and she joins them. All her meals are literally garbage from that point on.

Now let's say I encounter this young woman while possessing the knowledge that she actually is a princess. How do I convey this information? I can look at her eating trash and decide to point out how disgusting that makes her. You know, smack her on the hand and shout: "Don't do that! That's gross! You're eating so much garbage, and it's killing you!"

Her likely response would be shame, guilt, or condemnation. I would probably cause her to retreat to her fellow trash-eaters and consume more—deciding also to ignore anything I or someone like me would ever have to say again.

What if I could show her the truth? If I could pull out the papers that prove she's a daughter of the king, then she could start to see the higher reality. "Wait a minute; I can have a feast with anything I want to eat in the world? That's way better than this trash!" She will remember how a princess acts and begin to align with that.

And then, once we learn our identity, we get to show other people their created value, too! If that princess came back to the alley with sincere love in her eyes and arms full of royal food, I believe those who had been with her in poverty would be drawn to her crown. They saw what she was like when she ate trash; now the visible difference is staggering...and attractional. It's the new twist on the "beggar sharing bread" thought we talked about in Chapter 3.

Remember the movie *The Princess Diaries*? I mean, um, I didn't see it or anything...but I recall from the previews that Julie Andrews sat the girl down and with her classy British accent, declared: "This is how a prin-cess sips her soup." Then she demonstrated said sipping.[3] In the preview, at least, there was no scene of her screaming at the girl about how disgusting her sipping habits had become; no excessive focus on any of her current unprincesslike issues. She simply and graciously reminded her how a daughter of the king actually acts. This seems to me like a perfect parallel to how the Holy Spirit teaches us to be holy—only, He does it from the inside!

Believe it or not, there actually was a case of a "normal" girl from West Virginia, Sarah Culberson, who learned one day that her biological father ruled a community in Africa. *By birthright, she was a princess.* She described the scene when she entered her kingdom:

> They were amazing. There are about...300 people there to welcome you in the ceremony, singing, dancing, and I was like, "What did I do to deserve this?"[4]

Can you imagine her response to this unconditional love poured out simply based on who she was born to be? She chose to begin helping her people—starting a foundation that provides funding for schools, clean drinking water, economic opportunities, and other sustainable improvements to advance the community. "The title princess means responsibility, and that's what I'm taking on" she said.

For years, we've lectured the people in our churches— and, personally, teens in our youth ministries—about everything they are doing wrong. We've told them how a "good Christian" avoids certain sins and practices certain disciplines. And the results have been horrendous. Most studies agree that roughly only one out of every ten students that are *active* (not merely attending) in their church or youth group at the beginning of high school are still following Jesus upon graduating college.

What if instead of shaming them into avoiding typical teenage behavior and "doing devotions" like a Bible school professor in the name of being a better Christian, we spoke over them the truth of who God created them to be? Could it be that the unconditional love based on the fact that they were born to be sons and daughters of the King of kings burning in their hearts would compel them to advance His kingdom far more effectively?

I believe we have misunderstood the concept of preaching repentance. Most Christians who will read this book have seen one extreme or the other: the "turn or burn" ("eternity in hell awaits if you don't immediately change your sinful ways") kind of so-called outreach; or throwing out any mention of sin or a changed lifestyle due to fear of being labeled unloving.

But think about it in light of the princess example we just read. If we lead by telling someone they are a sinner, typically they will immediately go on the defensive, justify their actions, and harden their heart even more against us. But telling them to "go on eating their trash, God's cool with that, it's all about love" certainly doesn't help either.

What if preaching repentance is showing people the reason there is so much they hate about themselves, so much that frustrates them in life is *because they are not thinking or acting in line with who they actually are?* We have the documentation that shows the King is their Father, just waiting for us to "sign the adoption papers."

I don't hate anything about myself, thank you very much!

After seventeen years of therapy, I'm self-actualized, full of self-esteem, and rather pleased to live for self-indulgence.

I am aware that we all know people who claim to be "quite happy" with their life choices apart from God at this present time. But I also give this money-back guarantee that we all (even you, Maine homeschooler) know people who do recognize that something is definitely missing, even if they don't seem ready to acknowledge that it's Jesus. Those are the ones I'm most concerned about reaching here. I'm not saying don't pray for, share your faith with, or believe that God can reach group number one (Ray Comfort, for one, demonstrates how to do a fine job with them). But the fields are white unto harvest with people in the second category, and it's time to start winning for the Lamb the rewards of His suffering!

IDENTIFY YOURSELF!

Alan Hirsch relates this concept of victory through identity to the story of *The Wizard of Oz*:

> But through all their ordeals and in their final victory they discover that in fact they already have what they were looking for—in fact they had it all along. The Scarecrow is very clever, the Tin Man has real heart, and the Lion turns out to be very brave and courageous after all...what they needed was a situation that forced them to discover (or to activate) that which was already in them. They had what they were all looking for, only they didn't realize it.[5]

Wow, a Wizard of Oz reference. The teens in your youth ministry are blessed to have such a cutting-edge guy preaching to them every week. How was your Little House on the Prairie sermon series?

Hey, your first clever one! But I challenge you to come up with a more solid comparison. The whole movie consists of those characters *trying to discover what they already had.* Sound familiar? We can try to be holier through willpower, we can try to obtain victory over sin...and we can live in a state of discouragement and shame every time we fall short of these goals.

Or we can declare 1 Corinthians 15:57: "But let us give thanks to God! He wins the battle for us because of what our Lord Jesus Christ has done" (NIRV).

I am victorious...because God already won that battle through what Jesus did! With apologies to Keyser Söze, I honestly believe the greatest trick the devil ever pulled was to convince us that we still have to fight that battle. Let's not be unaware that he didn't stop twisting Scripture after Jesus stomped him in the desert. How many times have we heard 1 John 1:8, "If we claim to be without sin, we deceive ourselves and the truth is not in us," used as the definitive proof that we have to walk in constant confession of how messed up we are?

What if John is actually talking about self-righteousness? That is, claiming we do not need Jesus because we can achieve sinless perfection in our own strength. That would certainly be a deception. But the entire concept of #iamholy comes from the fact that *Christ* makes us free from sin. In fact, the verse right before that one states, "But if we walk in the light, as He is in the light, we have fellowship with one another, and the blood of Jesus, His Son, purifies us from all (or every) sin"! How could John tell us we are purified from all sin, and then go on to tell us we need to be continually conscious of it (as it has often been taught)?

"*Duh...what's sin? I don't need anybody's forgiveness!*" Sorry, bro—you're deceived and the truth isn't in you. We confess our need for redemption, our dependence upon Him to live holy. But if we've been cleansed from *every* sin, how can we still identify ourselves as sinners?

He goes on to say, "I write these things to you *so that you will not sin.*" But, hey, obviously we still have the ability to believe and act according to lies. If you do get into that, great news—we have an Advocate! But it's far better not to, and we all know willpower has pretty much been an epic fail, so let's stay focused on the fact that we're purified in Christ and live from that place of His firstlove!

Romans 6 tells us: "We died to sin, how can we live in it any longer? Or don't you know that all of us who were baptized into Christ Jesus were baptized into His death? We were therefore buried with Him through baptism into death in order that, just as Christ was raised from the dead through the glory of the Father, we too may live a new life" (vv. 2–4).

I heard someone say there exist two camps in modern evangelical circles regarding this issue. One basically says, "We are dead to sin because the Word says so." The other says, "Well, I obviously still sin. I know what the Bible says but I don't want to sound like I'm in denial or pretending I'm better than I actually am." The first mind-set has been expounded on throughout this whole book. It boils down to—through the power of Christ in us—bringing our experience to a place where it lines up with God's Word. The second one tries to bring His scriptural truth down to our level of current experience.

In these bodies, we have the ability to sin, sure. But

when we turn our hearts and put our faith in Jesus as our Lord and Savior, it no longer defines us! Let's compare sin to mud. Before salvation, we're attached to a chain in the mud, so to speak. We can stand to our feet at times, even brush ourselves off for a while to appear clean. But we never get far from it.

Now, after we're born again, God cuts that chain. In fact, He obliterates it from existence. Can we still choose to dive in the mud? Of course. But I would rather live clean. If (*not* when) I do believe the old lies and soil myself (haha) for a moment, I can instantly run to the industrial-strength fire hose of grace and become clean again!

But the Bible often mentions a battle we fight, or spiritual warfare. It has to be between our new, Jesus-following heart and our old, fleshly sin nature. Right?

I'm glad you asked. This is not only what I have always been taught, but what I preached in my own ministry for years. Our "sin nature" will always want to do what's wrong, selfish, against God's commands. But because I'm saved, my new "spirit" will always want to do what's right. If I pray and read the Bible more than I listen to worldly music and watch PG-13 movies, then my spirit will (probably) win.

Here's problem number one with that: Nobody has ever—consistently and long term—won that battle. That's the primary reason there's so much frustration and believing the lie that the life promised in Scripture is unattainable. Our identity has been based on how victorious we *feel*, and we often feel defeated, insecure, and fearful of our "dark side" being exposed.

Problem number two: The Bible doesn't say if we try really hard and get really good at "denying ourselves" then maybe one day Jesus will win and I'll be dead to sin. It says we *are* dead to sin. That's present and even past tense. If the Word says we died to sin and we can't live in it any longer, it really can't be what we battle against. It would be like fighting a corpse. Not much resistance there.

How Do We Put to Death... What's Already Dead?

The enemy has become an expert in *Weekend at Bernie's* type mischief. For those of you born after 1987 whose parents never introduced you to this cinematic classic, allow me. A man named Bernie dies at the beginning of the film. We get introduced to the main characters—two guys who would be in trouble if word gets out that he's dead but would really benefit from being associated with him as a live person. The entire rest of the movie (I am not making this up) consists of them propping up the dead body to do things like appear to drive a boat, attaching puppet-style strings to his arms and legs to make him wave and dance, and other such craziness that *convinces everyone they come in contact with that Bernie is not only alive, but wilder than ever!*[6]

OK, you can come back from YouTube now. Surreal, no? But that is spiritually what happens every time we grit our teeth and say, "Oh man, I feel like I just want to do this sin so bad. But I can't! I have to crucify that!" We may be able to—with much frustration—put off actually sinning for a while, but there's a reason nobody ever "wins" that battle: because we don't have to crucify what's already been crucified with Christ. The enemy is simply pulling a few strings to make the corpse seem alive again.

The battle—every battle, really—*is in our mind.* Am I going to believe the truth that I am dead to sin? Or the lie that part of me still wants to do these things? This is the place where we are truly "transformed by the renewing of our mind." It simply means making God's Word part of us by choosing to believe it over circumstances, temptations, and trials!

Romans 6 goes on to say (starting in verse 11): "Count yourselves dead to sin but alive to God in Christ Jesus." Let's recap: Jesus lives in me. He didn't merely save me from an eternity in hell,** but *He saved me from my sins!* I obey the Word and count myself dead to sin. I don't emphasize the fact that on this earth, I have the ability to sin. I focus on the truth that my actual identity is "alive to God in Christ Jesus!" He lives in me, and He is undefeated! As He is, so am I in this world.

One of the more fun declarations we've started making in our lives and ministry is "I win!"

Doubt, unbelief, fear? Nope…I win. Temptation to sin? You guessed it…I win.

I WIN AGAINST SIN: I AM HOLY

Ephesians 4:20–32 and all of Colossians 3 address the change from self-centered old sinful person to #iamholy born again new creation. They provide a pretty good description of what the Christian life looks like. But we need to unpack the concepts of "putting off" and "putting to death" the old nature. Specifically, we've talked already about recognizing the truth that our old nature is already dead, crucified with Christ. So how do we put to death what's already dead? How do we put off our old nature without getting into "works"? That is, what we have already

---

** Anybody else always want to follow up typing the word "hell" with a footnote that says, "Hebrew: *sheol*"—or is that just me?

acknowledged does not work: using willpower and trying really hard not to lie, curse, gossip, etc. So, what then?

Let's note that "put off" doesn't mean "manage." (Side note: has anyone ever had anyone recommend "anger management" as a solution? What's the thinking there? I wouldn't mind managing a car dealership, or an In-N-Out Burger. Why would you want to manage *anger*? I wanted mine gone, not "managed.") To "put off" these things means to put them off. Get rid of them forever.

Recognize the truth—that you were not created for those things. Get with God in prayer, declare that they are dead, and let Christ in you rise up. Surrender to Him with praise for the truth that His heart is in you. Thank Him that those things from your past have already been put to death and they have nothing to do with your created value![7]

I Win against Insecurity: I Am Fearless

Even Christians who sincerely believe that the Holy Spirit empowers us to share the gospel with people use a distortion of that truth to talk themselves out of it without admitting the real cause is their fear. I can't tell you how many times someone has left one of our gatherings determined to pray or even simply give an encouraging word to someone at school. A few days later, instead of powerful testimonies of God's love I hear excuses such as, "*Well, I just never got a green light*" or "*I didn't hear specifically from God to go talk to anybody.*" You want a green light? How about "Go into all the world and make disciples?" You didn't hear specifically from God? My friend, it doesn't get more specific than "You will receive power when the Holy Spirit comes on you, and you will *be my witnesses* to (in essence: your family, your school, your town, your nation, and) the ends of the earth!"

Jonathan, when faced with the choice of living a normal, powerless, "Christian" life (don't think so), or engaging the entire army of evil with one friend and one sword (of course, duh)—makes a pretty astonishing statement. Let's check 1 Samuel 14…he justifies his decision to advance God's kingdom with: "Perhaps the Lord will act in our behalf" (v. 6). Perhaps? Wouldn't you need a specific word, an angelic visitation, or a visiting prophet to confirm such a dangerous decision? Well, no. He knew God's revealed will, he knew nothing could hinder Him from saving, and he went and took the victory that was already promised! Twenty enemies fell, and all of God's people that had fallen away or were on the fence came back to His side! Because he believed—and acted upon—the truth, many were saved!

The teachings of Graham Cooke introduced me to a concept that changed everything. What if we always have a green light unless God specifically gives us a red one? Put the pitchforks down, I'm not talking about sin. But in taking a step of faith, giving financially to a godly cause, telling someone about the amazing love of Jesus, praying for someone to be healed—we already have the revealed will of God in Scripture. It's to do those things! How did Paul describe the amazing adventures he had with Barnabas? "It seemed good to me to do this." "It seemed good to us and the Holy Spirit to go here." The only time mentioned that God intervened directly? The one time He actually did give a red light. Acts 16:6—he was stopped by the Holy Spirit from going to Asia. That's it. The rest of the time he just did what he knew his Father wanted him to—even (especially?) if people tried to stop him. Why? Well, I believe the answer is found throughout Paul's writings, but specifically in Acts

17:28. "We are His offspring." He knew his place as a son, and therefore lived victory to victory!

DON'T KEEP THE FAITH. SHARE IT.

In his book (which I can't recommend enough) *Living For Another World*, Justin Kendrick explains:

> Everything rises and falls on identity. It seems that when God decides to break into our world and speak audibly, He always goes right to this issue of identity. When Jesus was being baptized by John the Baptist and the crowd heard an audible voice from Heaven...the voice simply dealt with Jesus' identity. It said "This is my beloved Son in whom I am well pleased."[8]

Now let's take a look at when Jesus starts His ministry. Watch how it's done by someone who knows their place as a son or daughter of the King. Jesus begins calling people to follow Him in John 1.

What do we know about Peter? Jesus is going to pour three years of His life into him, and he will still respond to situations with strife, cursing, violence, and some other choice words and decisions...culminating with the infamous denial of his Lord and best friend. Can you imagine what Peter's life looked like here, *before* spending large amounts of time being influenced by the holy and unconditionally loving King of kings?

And yet, Jesus doesn't speak to any of these rather large issues. He speaks to Peter's true identity. "You're not going to simply be one who listens (Simon), but I created you to be a rock (Peter)."

Then He comes to Nathaniel. Jesus has seen a vision

of him under a tree disparaging both Himself and His hometown. How would we have responded with that gift of supernatural knowledge? "Yo, I heard you dis my hometown under that tree. Nazareth High spanked you in football when I was there!" "Nothing good can come from there? How about this roundhouse kick?"

Jesus, however, doesn't even acknowledge the insult. He greets Nate with: "Here is a true Israelite, in whom there is nothing false" (John 1:47). What's He saying? "You'd better stop running your mouth before you get the facts. That won't suit you well if you're to be My disciple"? Nope. He says: "You were created to be a man of truth and honor. Follow Me and fulfill that destiny."

Do you notice something? In both of these cases Jesus says, "follow Me," but there's no mention of cleaning up their lives, only *hope*. This gospel message remains the same today. Jesus is still calling to His lost sons and daughters: "This is who I created you to be, and all you really need to do is believe in Me as your all in all. In a place of being consumed by My love, by My grace, lay down the things you weren't created for anyway and begin to walk as the rock that you are destined to be, faithful one."

This is how we share our faith! The truth that sets people free is not "accurate statements about their current issues." It's their created value! We awaken people to who God destined them to be.

Maybe some of us who weren't feeling the *Wizard of Oz* analogy can latch onto an awesome example from the recent show *Heroes*. Hiro Nakamura dreams of being a great hero, but his current reality is marked by insecurity, poor English-speaking skills, sloppy appearance (messy hair, glasses that won't stay on), and consistently making embarrassing mistakes. His supernatural gift is being able to stop or travel through time, but he either messes up every time he tries or uses it for something pointless like gambling. He constantly doubts and condemns himself, as do his co-workers and even his best friend.

Then, something happens that changes everything. Another character, Peter, is riding the subway when suddenly time stops. A man appears in the doorway and walks toward him. This man has perfect confidence, is dressed as a warrior—slicked back hair, samurai sword—and must be recognized as someone significant to his destiny. The first words out of his mouth? "My name is Hiro Nakamura."

It's Hiro from the future! Confident, perfect English . . . he has passed his tests and is boldly fulfilling his God-given destiny. When Peter tells present-day Hiro what he looks like in five years, it changes everything. He finds the sword and has his father teach him how to use it. He practices selflessness and using his gift to benefit others. And in the finale, he is the one to destroy the evil threat.[9]

We know God is not limited by time or space. Therefore, He already sees the men and women we have become five years down the road. Let's ask Him to show us a prophetic glimpse of who we already are, who He created us to be, and start living accordingly!

When we start following Jesus armed with this truth about our identity, we ensure that we will go from victory to victory. We become bold as we finally get a hold of "Whom shall I fear? Of whom shall I be afraid? If God is for me, nothing can stand against me!" Through Christ in us, the Father's ceremony of adoption, and the overflowing grace of the indwelling Holy Spirit, our new reality becomes #iamholy. And evangelism is simply sharing that truth with the people all around us. They were also created to host the presence of God as "sons and daughters revealed."

I encourage you to say it to yourself even now: "I win!" I am victorious!

Chapter 7
I AM POWERFUL

Early in my preaching days, I would encourage people with a paraphrase of St. Francis's famous quote: "Preach the gospel at all times, when necessary use words." I meant that we couldn't just run our mouths about Christianity; there had to be a lifestyle that lined up with what we are preaching.

However, as time went by I began to see that as a cop-out. People would think that if they just lived like a nice guy or girl, others near them would eventually come around to asking them about God. That rarely—if ever—works. In Lot's case (Gen. 19), it ended with massive destruction for himself and the people he vainly hoped his righteous lifestyle would reach. Jonah, on the other hand, didn't have much visible godly character, yet a whole city turned to God in repentance when he boldly opened his mouth to preach.

As I have learned #iamholy based on the Holy Spirit manifesting through me, I have gone back to endorsing the St. Francis quote...from a totally different mind-set. The Bible asks the question, "How will they know, unless we tell them?" It's the Word that ultimately pierces people's hearts and leads to salvation, and it's Christians who are called to preach the Word in and out of season. But all the "telling" in the world won't win us the right to be heard consistently unless our lives are also clearly preaching the gospel.

Banning Liebscher addresses this need for a life that "delivers the goods" in regards to the power of God. He compares a powerless Christian life to a vacuum salesperson who throws dirt on the carpet before the demonstration of how amazing their product is...only, they didn't bring a vacuum:

> *"What are you doing? Why did you just throw dirt on my carpet?"*
>
> "Well, I wanted to let you know that the vacuum cleaner I represent could clean up that dirt in two minutes without leaving a trace on your carpet."
>
> *"What! Where is your vacuum cleaner? Clean this up!"*
>
> "Well, I didn't actually bring my vacuum cleaner with me. But trust me, if I had brought it I would have blown your mind by how powerful it is. So, would you like to purchase one?"
>
> *"No! Go away!"*
>
> It is somewhat of a silly illustration, but that is how many of us learned to evangelize—words with no power. We would highlight to people their sins and problems and tell them Jesus is the answer to their situation, but we would never *demonstrate* that truth. This makes us ineffective in convincing people of that reality.[1]

POWERFUL LIVING

We often equate "power" to supernatural signs, wonders, and miracles. (Don't worry, we'll get to those.) I hold that in our desire to see the spectacular we miss a supernatural act of God that is just as powerful. First Peter 3:9: "Do not repay evil with evil or insult with insult, but with blessing, because to this you were called so that you may inherit a blessing." How often has this been our reality? It fascinates me how people take Christian clichés and use them to justify being worldly instead of Christlike. Jesus said: "turn the other cheek." We say: "Christians should be servants, but not doormats!" Why do we say this? Because someone is personally offending us (proving we still love our lives not unto death), and darn it, we're going to stand up for our rights.

Please understand, I'm not talking about situations like a legitimately off-base review at work or grade at school. You don't just "release forgiveness" and take the bad report. We can take a completely honoring position toward the authority figure and respectfully show the details that back up our point.

I'm talking about "defending yourself" when your BFF runs up to you in the school hallway and reports that "So-and-so called you a bleeping bleep." Or when the woman at the watercooler informs you what Jenny from the office down the hall really thinks about you. We often slam them right back to prove we're not a doormat. The world trained us that this is the only way to show strength.

Is anybody else sick and tired of letting sin against us produce sin in us? Instead of coming back with "No, *she's* a bleeping bleep," how about, "Man, I love her so much. Jesus, I just pray that You bless her today. Show her how amazing You created her to be"? Stop crying because of other people, and start crying *for* them![2]

We are seeing people get a hold of #iamholy and begin letting the Holy Spirit in them—instead of the wisdom of the world—lead their response to evil and insults.

One young man had someone at school basically pull out every insult imaginable toward his brother who was, at the time, serving a prison sentence. One year earlier, the outcome would have been a punch to the cabeza. After ten months of praying and practicing in the grace of God, he chose to let Jesus take this one. He instantly sensed God's heart toward this young man, released forgiveness, and blessed him...to the astonishment of the other students at the table. He has already begun to inherit the blessing for such radical obedience.

Another seventeen-year-old young woman from the Rising had a taste of the cyberbullying most of the older generation is just starting to learn about. An anonymous schoolmate on a social networking site began persistently insisting she kill herself. Her initial reaction was, of course, to repay insult with insult. She composed a message out of hurt and anger, and was just about to send it. Then the still small voice in her spirit reminded of her passion not to let sin against us produce sin in us. She immediately erased her message and replaced it with one of gracious love. This anonymous bully who had earlier sent six straight messages telling her to end her life now responded with shocked gratitude, saying how much he needed to hear that and apologizing for his earlier sentiments.

Come on! We don't need to pretend people will always respond so well right away, but we already established that love is the only thing that will change problem behavior... *and we are starting to see it happen.* They are seeing our good deeds, and God is glorified! This is a power-filled lifestyle that we enter into by grace through faith.

POWERFULLY SHARING OUR FAITH

As we start living our lives by the power of the Holy Spirit, we begin to see eyes open to the fact that something is different about us. What about when it is time to "use words"?

What the Lord showed me about "relationship evangelism"

There was a young man in my youth ministry who had a real passion for the things of God, but balked whenever we would go out in public and share our faith with people. He finally told me he really wasn't into the whole "praying for people at the mall" thing. His call was to be a "relational evangelist." That is, he would build friendships with other teens and in the context of comfortable conversations, share his faith.

I could have led with "Um, what does that have to do with anything? Shouldn't that be happening anyway?" Instead, I got real. In fact, I informed him how I personally gravitate toward that sort of outlook and had made that same statement to God a few years earlier. You may have heard (or thought) some of the same excuses I used. "Well, if I share Jesus with someone on the street, how do I know if they really mean it? How do I know they'll ever go to church again? I'm going to be a relational evangelist, God. That way, I'll see a lot more lasting fruit."

Let me remind you, I have never heard the audible voice of God. The vast majority of the time when I "hear from" Him, it is simply a sense in my heart of what He is saying.

There have been, however, several occasions when I have felt like He was speaking sentences directly to my heart.

Also, if you haven't noticed yet, I believe God is the most kind, loving, gentle, encouraging Person I have ever met…and it's not even close.

That's to prepare you for this next explanation: I have found that the Lord speaks to different people in different ways. I believe it's because He loves how He made each of us unique, and delights in relating to us in ways we are familiar with. (Obviously He is God. He can and does communicate however He desires. I just happened to notice a way He often chooses to do so.)

Every word in this book has been covered in prayer that God's love will be apparent. You may have noticed, however, that I tend to be direct and to the point at times. Indeed, my Father will often speak to me that way as well.

That being said, here's how it went down. I made my comment about preferring relational evangelism and sat back, quite proud of myself. I remember to this day the words God spoke to my heart:

"How's that working out for you?"

No condemnation, no accusation, just a direct question that went straight to the core of my choice. I had to admit I had not led someone to Jesus outside of a youth ministry setting in over a year.

Again, the relational evangelism should be a given. But now that I bring tangible ministry that comes from a heart that knows #iamholy everywhere I go, I found a good comparison point.

CLOCKS

Let's say someone who doesn't know anything or is completely opposed to Jesus is at 12:00 on an old-fashioned analog clock. (And yes, the teens in your church will get the comparison. There's likely one in your youth room. Hey now!) One o'clock—an "hour" later—represents their moment of salvation. Everyone moves from twelve to one at different paces. Someone could encounter God in a powerful moment and do the whole hour at once. More often, exposure to the Light through interactions with God's people moves them a few minutes closer.

My friend "Wendell" started, like all of us, at twelve noon. I see him two or three times a year. Over the past thirteen years, he has seen Christ at work in me. And every time I see him, he gets closer. Early on, he literally got angry when I brought up anything about God or the Bible. As time went on, he would put up with a little discussion here or there on spiritual subjects. Then, he would even bring up questions or observations along those lines. One of the most recent times I spoke to him, he actually asked me for prayer and godly advice!

So, it's safe to say that relational evangelism can be effective. Wendell can safely be described at approximately 12:30 on his symbolic clock.

One day at my former job, a woman came up to me in tears. She said her fiancé, a military man stationed overseas, had been cleared for two weeks leave. That morning, she expected to pick him up in a few hours and begin a week of blissful re-connection...but she was informed his leave had been delayed by more than a day. This totally messed up their travel plans (which would cost them quite a bit of money to change—money they didn't have). She knew I had a relationship with Jesus and asked if I could pray. I did. She thanked me.

Then, an hour later as I was working at my computer, she ran up and hugged me from behind. "Bruce is coming home tonight!" she practically shouted, "Your prayer worked! Thank you, thank you, thank you!" Guess who also went from twelve to twelve-thirty? The difference is thirteen years versus thirty seconds.

P.S.: Here's a tweet from the young man I mentioned, posted last week (August 2013), a little over a year after our "just a relational evangelist" conversation:

> *Going to the mall to spread the love of God and show the world what they're made for!*

POWERFUL PRAYING

Let's think about how this applies to praying powerful prayers. Jesus has several teachings on this that, at first glance, seem to contradict each other. In Luke 11 and 18, He speaks about the importance of persistence in prayer. Basically, if you don't just ask once but continue to seek, God will grant what we "cry out for day and night."

Yet, the Word also teaches on more than one occasion that when we pray, we are to "believe that we have received" (Mark 11:24, Matt. 21:22, Mark 9:23).

How can we reconcile this apparent paradox? If we ask more than once, do we not believe God heard and answered us the first time? If we put our faith in the promise that He did honor our request the first time, do we throw out the imperative to pray with persistence?

In Luke 11, the friend had the three loaves of bread in his possession. In Luke 18, the judge had the ability to grant justice. Both parables are followed with the revelation of a God who loves giving His chosen children good gifts.

My practice of "beg God over and over again until maybe He has sympathy and gives me what I'm persistently asking for" should have been so clearly in opposition to actual faith, but I continued to operate that way for years.

I think many of us have misunderstood faith. I lived and preached for years that if you really believed with all your heart that God heard your prayer and had a strong conviction that He would answer, then you were praying with faith. I now see that actually defines praying with *hope*.

Really, faith in prayer is declaring the answer that we have already been given in the spiritual realm. Thanking God for His promise and asking that His kingdom come and will be done through us as He gives us our daily bread.

The closer we get to our Lord through "prayer and practice" the more clear His will becomes to us, and the more powerfully we can declare it over our lives. I encourage everyone to go before Him every morning and ask as the disciples did in John 1: "Where are You staying today? What do You want to accomplish in and through me in this hour?"

SUPERNATURAL SIGNS AND WONDERS

One of the truly cool things about the church's return to unity is that we can all team up around the essentials of the faith. We can disagree respectfully on what we term "non-essentials."

For example, some believe that the gifts of the Holy Spirit as described in 1 Corinthians—healings, miracles, prophecy, and the rest—operate through God's people today. Others believe they stopped occurring after the initial Acts of the Apostles.

Regardless of what one believes about these gifts of the Holy Spirit, we can agree Jesus is Lord and join hands to tell the world about Him.

When I look at the whole of Scripture, examples from church history, and the difference in my own life with and without them, I personally believe these gifts of the Holy Spirit are for us today. There's a time for a John the Baptist type ministry—one that preaches truth with no miracles—but we want the ministry of our ultimate example, Jesus. One big confirmation is that these things are happening on pretty much a weekly basis in our youth ministry, glory to God.

As we grow in Him, we learn true humility and lose the need to run our mouths. However, when the Holy Spirit comes on us with the gift of faith, we experience what it is like to speak with power.

A high school freshman once showed up at a Rising invite night with his foot in a boot. (I had to pull out a rare display of public pastoral correction when I made him stop trying to join the dodgeball game.) Two hours later, another freshman asked if he could declare something. In front of everyone, he shared what God had shown him that evening, then turned to the injured teen, saying, "...and it's about time we pray for *you*." Immediately, faith rose up in me. I asked the group of about thirty students (many of whom were unchurched) if anyone believed God could supernaturally heal. About twenty raised their hands. Again, this was all Holy Spirit, because the next thing I said came out like, "everyone who doesn't believe, that's cool...you will in about thirty seconds." Everyone's heart exploded in worship toward God when, after being prayed for, this young man took off his cast and started *walking normally with no pain.*

We talked for years about how we wanted to see the healing and supernatural words of prophecy in the midst of our gatherings. We glimpsed these things over the first few years and our faith has increased, but never again will we "try" to have enough faith to see Him move in those ways.

Now, when someone comes in with a physical affliction, it's simple. We explain how God loves us, and He talks to His kids. He told me He wants to give you this gift.

When we look at what the Word says about this subject, it becomes plain as day. First Corinthians 12 Talks about the gifts of the Holy Spirit, and how we should eagerly desire them. But Paul almost seems to interrupt himself to explain that they have to be desired in the more excellent way. The purpose of these gifts is *love!*

One of the most powerful seven-day stretches of ministry in my life occurred on a short-term mission trip to Scotland.

We saw supernatural signs and wonders every day. Dozens of people that we encountered experienced salvations, instant healings—both physical and emotional—as well as some pretty unique happenings that can only be described as the hand of God. Our boldness increased by the hour. One day we had just finished ministering God's love to a precious lost daughter on the street, when we looked up to see the tail end of a funeral service. The pallbearers were exiting the church with the casket, and family and friends began streaming out behind them.

I'm telling you, the three of us simultaneously started taking a few steps toward the deceased, all thinking the same thing: Resurrection! Then, a brief hesitation. We exchanged glances and grins, shaking our heads like Colonel Rhodes from the first Iron Man movie when he saw the extra suit hanging up on his way out the door: "Next time, baby."

It was awesome. And yet when I got home to America, these signs and wonders ceased happening on a daily basis. We saw some cool things in our youth ministry gatherings, but I went months without seeing anything externally supernatural in my daily life.

When I asked myself why, I came up with what seemed like a pretty solid answer. While on the mission field, my faith and expectation were sky-high. I believed God would move through us, and He honored that faith by doing exactly that. Back in America, a place where I had rarely seen signs and wonders in daily life, my faith and expectation adjusted accordingly. Therefore, so did the results.

There may be an element of accuracy to that, thought— but if so, it was simply a symptom of the actual cause.

I was, every moment while in Scotland, captivated to my core by the all-consuming love of God. I loved and pursued His presence in personal and group worship, devoured the Word multiple times per day, and embraced true Acts-style fellowship with the locals. The street and church ministry came from a place of a heart that burned with passion to see His name glorified and His love spread like wildfire.

And when I got back to America, though I still "loved God," that natural flow stopped because "life" got in the way.

Thinking back to that trip, I suppose He actually gave me a special sneak preview of what the post-grace conversion life would look like! Responsibilities of life, circumstances, temporary trials—no more do these get in the way of being loved by my Father and letting His love flow out of me from that place.

The Million Dollar Question: But What If Someone Doesn't Get Healed When We Pray?

I don't yet see everyone I pray for get 100 percent healed instantly. But I do see healings on a regular basis when I pray. So does my wife. So do the teens at the Rising. I've heard it said that someone may not get healed when we pray for them, but the percentage that do will be much higher than if we don't pray! I don't recall a single instance in the Bible where someone came to Jesus for prayer and they didn't get healed.

"Well, that's a shaky comparison. He was God, and I'm not!"

We're way past that excuse. Through dozens of scriptures quoted in this book we've established, confirmed, and set into foundation the truth that He lives in and through us.

Dan Mohler often addresses our tendency to rewrite theology to fit ours instead of seeking to bring our experience up to the reality of the Bible. If I can paraphrase, let's stop worrying about if our prayers are going to be effective (James 5 already says they are), and start focusing on the finished work of Jesus—by His stripes we have been healed!

There is no pressure when we pray for someone to be healed. It's not based on how we pray, but our faith in *who God is*. We can adopt Wigglesworth's life message and just believe! All we do is show His love to people and put ourselves in a position for Him to use our prayers to bring healing, freedom, and encouragement.

Remember, the "I am" comes from "I AM." Tim Whitbeck compares praying for someone to telling them about an upcoming all-star basketball demonstration. You would never think, "What if they don't dunk? I'd be humiliated!" Why? Because that's not your part. You know that they will do some amazing dunks, because that's the nature of those guys. If for whatever reason they do not, did you fail? Not at all. That was their responsibility.[3]

Here's what our youth ministry family has recently come to realize: we cannot make the situation worse. We often justify not praying for any non-Christians because we think, for example, if God does not heal them then they will think that God doesn't heal. Gasp! Guess what? They already think God doesn't heal! Or, "I really feel prompted to tell that stranger at the mall that Jesus loves them, but that would probably make them think Christians are freaks, and I don't want to be responsible for that." Newsflash: *They already think Christians are freaks.* Or even, "If I get too hardcore about God, my friends will talk about me as soon as I leave the room." Sister, if you don't know they already do exactly that...I don't know what to tell you. The gossip directed toward you has been happening from your "friends" for quite some time now. Why not get a heavenly reward too while they're at it?

Reminder: Powerful living is not a resolution you make in order to get a heavenly reward. This will naturally flow from your life when you're captivated by the love of God. Every day, let Him enforce the truth that #iamholy. We know how to do this—develop a love for His Word, pray and listen, encourage your spirit by faith, praise and worship, get around other Christians who burn with a passion for Jesus, respond to God's greatness instead of circumstances, come on! You cannot be touched consistently by His love and *not* let that overflow out of you to impact the souls around you.

Again, we cannot make the situation worse. Know it's always God's will to heal, do your part and step out in faith—and if for whatever reason a healing doesn't take place, guess what? They (who likely already didn't believe in healing and thought Christians were weird) now know that someone cares about them enough to lift their situation up in prayer. That might be the biggest "miracle" they've ever experienced.

As we begin to pray powerfully, our life will start to manifest the power of sanctification. Instead of reacting to situations or people with toxic emotions, we will instead respond according to Christ living in us. And, if we really want to follow Paul's encouragement to pursue the gifts of the Holy Spirit, we just may enter the greatest adventure of our lives. Because God is the most powerful being in the universe for all eternity, as His sons and daughters—in all the ways discussed in this chapter and so many more—we are powerful, too.

Chapter 8

I AM HUMBLE

True humility is not an abject, groveling,
self-despising spirit; it is but a right
estimate of ourselves as God sees us.
—Tryon Edwards

Humble yourselves, therefore,
under God's mighty hand, that He
may lift you up in due time.
—1 Peter 5:6

Psh! "I AM *powerful*" before "*I am humble*"? *I'd say you're anything but!*

I don't even have any more snappy comebacks. I did intentionally put this chapter last because humility is different than the happiness, power, and everything else we mentioned earlier. All those other facets of #iamholy come directly from God, and we simply partner with Him by faith and begin to walk them out. But the Word doesn't tell us to ask for or receive humility from God. It says *humble yourself in the sight of the Lord* (see James 4:10). Obviously the grace to do so still comes from the Holy Spirit in us, but practicing this will look a bit different than the traits from the previous seven chapters.

Loving others, for example, is an intentional choice...but it's based upon the love God has deposited into us. Nowhere do I see anything about God putting humility into us. Christ humbled Himself, and we are called to do the same. It's a laying down of our lives, our "rights," everything the world trained us to be selfish in. Humility does not mean an absence of confidence; if anything, the most humble people become the most truly confident in who God is in and through us.

In fact, false humility is nothing more than pride with a cheap Halloween mask on. Do we really think God gets multiples of glory based on the amount of times we announce that we are "just a broken vessel"? I am humble, desperate, and dependent on God because He showed me my created value as a son. Of course I'm a hot mess without Him. He has always seen me fulfilling my potential as a man who turned my heart away from the mess and ran to Him for grace. If I declare myself *just* a broken vessel, that seems to cheapen the fact that Jesus paid the highest price to redeem me! Dan Mohler reminds us that we wouldn't pay $100,000.00 for a $10,000.00 car! How much more valuable am I in His sight that Christ would shed His blood for me?[1]

True humility means realizing what we talked about way back in the introduction. It's all about God. I choose to live out the truth that "my" agenda, my selfish ways, any human desire for glory *died with Jesus when I repented and was born again.* I humble myself by choosing to live transparently before my wife, my pastor, my tribe...pretty much everyone, for that matter. I assure you, this was not always the case.

PRIDE AND PREJUDICE. WELL, PRIDE AND MORE PRIDE, ACTUALLY.

Ever since I became a youth pastor, I preached what I was taught—the importance of being open and honest in our walk of faith. I probably preached against hypocrisy too, which made me pretty engrossed in a double standard.

Personally, I kept a huge wall up. This especially held true when ministering in a large group setting. All my personal stories centered on outcomes where I came out looking good. I told them it was OK to wrestle with doubts but put forth the image of a man who only operated in faith, 24/7. I even remember making a decision not to smile too much because people would think I was weird or phony. When I *did* smile, people would know I meant it and would feel honored. Man, I fell into deception on that one. Looking back, I realize that many hope-filled messages I delivered came across as angry and condemning due to my awful case of "super serious face."

I now admit that pride and keeping walls up was the case not only when ministering to a crowd, but with the young leaders I mentored as well.

I wanted them to aspire to a victorious Christian life. I wanted them to catch my passion, vision, and boldness without having to get near my doubts and hidden sin.

The biggest one of those hidden sins was pride. Never the kind of pride that thought, "Hey, look at me, I'm a hot-shot preacher that can inspire teens in their faith." From the earliest days of my initial salvation, I knew the grace of God as it related to ability and success in ministry.

This was the kind of pride that pretended I *personally* was doing OK without help from Jesus. During one four-month period where I oversaw three amazing ministries, my walk with Him basically dried up. Yes, I prayed and read the Bible almost every day—but it all related to the next youth service or camp decision. The ministry didn't miss a beat. From all appearances, everything still thrived. Lives were changing; Bible clubs were popping up at almost every school in town. Even the school police officer at the most problematic public middle school asked one of the kids' parents for my contact info. You know, to say: "I don't know what you're doing at that there youth group…but please keep it up." We saw teens "get saved" virtually every week. The group went from eleven students my first night to just under one hundred students fourteen months later. It was the place to be, not just for fun and socializing, but to encounter God in a way that made a real impact. It was every youth pastor's dream.

And by the end of that time, I had to acknowledge that Jesus and I had become strangers. That only applied to my side of the relationship, of course, but as the great theologian Doc Holliday said, "My hypocrisy knew no bounds."

I crashed and burned hard. For the first time in my *life*— even the "before Christ" days—I sunk into depression. I had to approach my pastor and ask to step down from ministry. I turned my heart back to God immediately, but did not feel His presence for almost two full months.

Little did I know, this was a preview of my victorious life to come. Where joy, peace, even hope itself are not dependent on external circumstances or internal feelings but on the truth of God's promises. Because I didn't "feel" Him, all I could do was walk back and forth in my apartment meditating on and declaring promises from His Word. Things like: "In my anguish I cried to the Lord…and He answered by setting me free. The Lord is with me; I will not be afraid. What can man do to me? The Lord is with me; He is my helper. I will look in triumph on my enemies." Day after day, I felt nothing. And every day, I continued to declare His truth over myself. "Out of the depths I cry to you, O Lord; O Lord, hear my voice. Let Your ears be attentive to my cry for mercy. If You, O Lord, kept a record of sins, who could stand? But with You, there is forgiveness; therefore You are feared."

I continued to feel absolutely nothing. Yet without a tangible sense of comfort, my heart *knew* more and more every day that the Holy Spirit was my Comforter. As Smith Wigglesworth often stated: the Bible said it, I believed it…and that settled it.

In His wisdom (and after hundreds of gracious offers to repent of my pride and be changed from the inside out), God allowed my actions to have their rightful consequences. I stopped depending on Him, and the result was total emotional burnout. But when I humbled myself, He began to speak to me about sonship. About how I had defined myself by having a thriving ministry, but He had always willed my satisfaction to come from the revelation of "You're My son, and I love you."

I once heard a pastor denounce Wigglesworth's statement from above by preaching a whole message on "It doesn't matter if I believe it or not; if the Word says it, that settles it!" Of course, in the grand scheme of absolute truth, that is a correct statement. But we've already seen for the lost son or daughter who doesn't believe, telling them they're wrong and we're right doesn't settle anything except the fact that they won't be back to finish the discussion anytime soon. Our amazing God designed it so our belief plays a pivotal role in this whole process. The Word said the same thing as I was sinking into burnout and depression; it wasn't until I chose to believe (without feeling a thing) that the issue became settled in my soul. One of the ultimate acts of humility is laying down what I feel and honoring what He said as the higher reality.

#IAMHOLY Was Preceded by "I Am Humble"

A man of God prayed over me in my first year of youth ministry: "Continue to take the low seat. Your place as a prophet will come from the place of being a son—and that will come from first being a servant." I put off the "low seat" and "servant" part for years. I was gifted and anointed, and that was enough, right? When I finally embraced the low seat of a servant, the revelation of sonship followed almost immediately afterward. That's right—the grace conversion that launched almost everything written in this book came after I decided to humble myself before God and man. I submitted to my father in the faith and some other spiritual authorities that I didn't necessarily agree with at the time. That part wasn't especially pleasant. But Jesus was right there in the center of it. And His grace carried me, shaped me, and gave me everything I needed for that season.

I'm still learning to walk as a son. I actually believe God has said that Becca and I are in a five-year period of testing. Here's the thing: It's fun and exciting and He is moving like crazy in the midst of it all. Yes, it includes "suffering," but that really just means the "pain" that comes from cutting off the false life I was giving to things that were already dead.

Only God's unconditional love can consistently—and increasingly—produce the response of humbling myself. The fact that the King of the universe chooses to be in intimate relationship with me absolutely keeps me choosing the low seat. The knowledge that He uses me daily in such powerful ways—and never for a moment reminds me that based on my performance I don't deserve it (that's why there's no "I am unworthy" chapter. It may be accurate, but it's never His focus in our relationship so it's never mine): this revelation is what keeps me on my face, completely dependent on His grace.

CONCLUSION

We started with "Be holy, for the Lord your God is holy." We unpacked how that actually starts to look. "God is holy, therefore since I have turned my heart away from my old ways and put my faith in Him—through the finished work of Jesus and the Holy Spirit in me—I am holy!" Once we catch that revelation, the daily process of maturity and improving character becomes natural (and often even, dare I say, fun).

I appreciate you going on this walk with me. I'm excited to hear stories about how this starts to manifest in people's lives as we search the Word and seek God in prayer on these truths. The hashtag in the title wasn't just a cool gimmick. We did it intentionally to facilitate the movement God has already started out of frustration, guilt, and condemnation into the holy lives we've always longed for. Please look me up on Facebook and Twitter (MikeMassl) and let me know your journeys into becoming more loved, loving, happy, passionate, victorious, powerful, and humble. #iamholy—Thank You, Lord!

NOTES

CHAPTER 1: I AM HOLY?

1.   Dan Mohler, *"Your New Identity"* podcast, Christ Community Church, June 29, 2012.

2.   Derek Levendusky, *Discipleship by Grace* (Potter, KS: 5 Stone Publishing, 2009), 103.

3.   Justin Kendrick, Brave Generation Conference, April 13, 2013; Boxborough, MA.

4.   Ibid.

5.   Ibid.

CHAPTER 2: I AM LOVED

1.   Dan Mohler, Twitter post, May 16, 2013, https://twitter.com/danmohler.

2.   Paul Washer, Twitter post, May 20, 2013, https://twitter.com/paulwasher.

3.   Dan Mohler, *"Your New Identity"* podcast, Christ Community Church, June 29, 2012.

4.   Derek Levendusky, *Discipleship by Grace* (Potter, KS: 5 Stone Publishing, 2009), 159.

5.   Ibid.

6.   Ibid.

CHAPTER 3: I AM LOVING

1.   Dan Mohler, *"Your New Identity"* podcast, Christ Community Church, June 29, 2012.

2.   Ibid.

3.   *Father of Lights*, film, directed by Darren Wilson (2012: Wanderlust Productions).

4.   Wallace Henley, *Revolution, Confronting the New World Disorder*, (Houston: Encourager Media, 1995), 249.

5.   Alan Hirsch, *The Forgotten Ways* (Grand Rapids, MI: Brazos Press, 2006), 33.

6.   Ibid.

CHAPTER 4: I AM HAPPY

1.   Derek Levendusky, *Discipleship by Grace* (Potter, KS: 5 Stone Publishing, 2009), 68.

2.   "Why Smiling Makes People Feel Happier," *The British Psychological Society*, February 8, 2012, http://www.bps.org.uk/news/why-smiling-makes-you-feel-happier (accessed December 12, 2013).

3.   Dan Mohler, *"Your New Identity"* podcast, Christ Community Church, June 29, 2012.

4.   Leon Van Rooyen, *The Glorious Church* (Tampa, FL: Global Ministries and Relief, 2005), 82.

CHAPTER 5: I AM DEVOTED

1.   Banning Liebscher, *Jesus Culture: Living a Life That Transforms the World* (Shippensburg, PA: Destiny Image Publishers, Inc., 2009), 116.

2.   Harold Chadwick, *How to be Filled with Spiritual Power: Based on the Miracle Ministry of John G. Lake* (Gainesville, FL: Bridge-Logos, 2006), 54.

3.   Liebscher, *Jesus Culture*, 113.

CHAPTER 6: I AM VICTORIOUS

1.   Camp Bethel (Red Hook, NY) promo video, 2005.

2.   Gilbert K. Chesterton. BrainyQuote.com, Xplore Inc, 2014. http://www.brainyquote.com/quotes/quotes/g/gilbertkc104748.html, accessed January 2, 2014.

3.   *The Princess Diaries*, film, directed by Garry Marshall (2001; Burbank, CA: Walt Disney Pictures).

4.   "Suburban Girl Finds Out She's A Princess" ABC News, September 19, 2006, http://abcnews.go.com/GMA/story?id=2462250&page=1#.UbQGJejD_IU (accessed December 12, 2013).

5.   Hirsch, *The Forgotten Ways*, 21.

6.   *Weekend at Bernie's*, film, directed by Robert Klane (1989; Harnett, NC: Gladden Entertainment).

7.   Dan Mohler, *"Your New Identity"* podcast, Christ Community Church, June 29, 2012.

8.   Justin Kendrick, *Living for Another World* (New York: Holyfire Ministries, 2009), page 72.

9.   *Heroes*, NBC, 2006–2010.

CHAPTER 7: I AM POWERFUL

1.　Liebscher, *Jesus Culture: Living a Life That Transforms the World*, 202–203.

2.　Dan Mohler, "*Your New Identity*" podcast, Christ Community Church, June 29, 2012.

3.　Tim Whitbeck, personal conversation with the author.

CHAPTER 8: I AM HUMBLE

1.　Dan Mohler, "*Your New Identity*" podcast, Christ Community Church, June 29, 2012.

ABOUT THE AUTHOR

Mike Massé has been in ministry for 17 years, and is known as a powerful speaker to audiences of teens and adults alike. He has ministered various places across the nation and overseas, but primarily in the Northeastern United States. Mike has a passion to lead people into victorious lives through mentoring and life coaching. He is currently on the pastoral staff at River of Life in Tolland, CT. Mike and his wife Becca oversee a youth movement called The Rising, and they have three children: Micah, Josiah Talon, and To Be Determined (in utero as of this printing).

CONTACT THE AUTHOR

Website: www.iamholy.net
Twitter: MikeMass1
Email: iamholy23@gmail.com